UNBILLABLE HOURS

A TRUE STORY

"Graham's telling of the overwrought work environment at Latham Watkins brings John Grisham's The Associate to real life."

- New York Journal of Books

"Unbillable Hours is the story of the intersection--or more accurately the collision--between Graham's pri vileged yet unhappy life in the law and Rocha's harsh yet hopeful quest for vindication and freedom. It's a true story that has the perfect arc of a good legal thriller, and the droll humor of a good stand-up routine to boot."

- The American Lawyer

"Like Grisham, Only Better..."

- AOL

"It would be difficult to find a fictional legal thriller as low-key yet as engrossing as Unbillable Hours...
Filled with captivating portraits, the book provides a riveting look at gang politics, courtroom deceptions and the behind-the-scenes drama of big law firms."

- Rice University Magazine

UNBILLABLE HOURS

A TRUE STORY

Ian Graham

Electric Avenue

PUBLISHING

Published by Electric Avenue Publishing, a division of Electric Avenue Entertainment, LLC.
1113 Electric Avenue, 13
Venice, CA90291

Library of Congress Cataloging-in-Publication Data

Graham, Ian, 1974-
Unbillable hours : a true story / by Ian Graham.
p. cm.
ISBN 9780692214305
1. Rocha, Mario, 1979---Trials, litigation, etc. 2. Trials (Murder)--California.
3. Judicial error--California. 4. Graham, Ian--Biography. 5. Lawyer--California--
Biography. 6. Latham & Watkins. I. Title.
KF225.R63G73 2010
340.092--dc22
[B]
2009045813

Printed in the United States of America

10 9 8 7 6 5 4 3 2 1

ISBN-13: 9780692214305

Every saint has a past
and every sinner has a future.

—Oscar Wilde

CONTENTS

Acknowledgments ix

Introduction xi

1. I'm Going to Prison 1
2. Make Me an Offer 11
3. Welcome Back 31
4. Baby Sharks 41
5. Monkey Scribe 53
6. Murder in the Barrio 67
7. Dreams of Freedom 79
8. God Boxed Me In 91
9. Right to Counsel 105
10. Denied 113
11. You're Going to Save His Life 127
12. You'll Do Fine 137

13. Nice to Meet You. 143

14. These Deficiencies Have Cost Me. 153

15. Strike Two 169

16. As Good As It Gets 183

17. A Lengthy Process 197

18. What's This? 205

19. A Strongly Worded Decision 213

20. A Good Question 231

Postscript. 239

ACKNOWLEDGMENTS

THE ROLES OF Mario Rocha, Sister Janet Harris, and Bob Long in making this story possible will be obvious to the reader. I hope it will also be obvious that I am grateful for knowing and working with them. I am grateful also to Susan Koch and Jeff Werner for creating the excellent documentary film *Mario's Story*, which shows the strength and endurance of the people involved and serves as an invaluable record of their efforts.

I would like to thank my agent, Rafael Sagalyn, for believing I could turn this story into a book and my editor, Don Fehr, for the advice and guidance that helped me do so. Thanks also to Michelle Ward, whose encouragement and honest opinion helped keep me going. And finally, I want to thank my parents, Rosemond and Tom, for not laughing when I said I wanted to quit law practice and write a book, and for their invaluable counsel without which this book would not have been possible.

INTRODUCTION

At a time when I thought I knew what I wanted, but still had a lot to learn, I became a lawyer. And it was my good luck to land my first job out of law school at Latham & Watkins, one of the world's largest and most prestigious law firms.

This book is an account of my five years as an associate at Latham in Los Angeles. It is not a novel. But because it was written by a lawyer, a few caveats are in order.

Latham & Watkins is a real law firm. Mario Rocha, Sister Janet Harris, and Bob Long are real people. Those are their names, and the case that bound us together happened the way it is described here. A lot of the testimony and dialogue come directly from court transcripts. Some other conversations are from memory, mine and other people's, and so are necessarily approximations, accurate, I believe, in content and tone.

Mario Rocha's case built up a huge public file as it was argued back and forth in at least eight courtrooms over twelve years. The case received a lot of press and was the subject of an award-winning documentary film, *Mario's Story*.* Many people on all sides—prosecutors, defendants, witnesses, defense

---

**Mario's Story*, produced by Susan Koch and directed by Susan Koch and Jeff Werner, won the audience award for best documentary at the 2006 Los Angeles Film Festival. *www.mariostory.org*

attorneys—have already been identified publicly with the case. Their real names are used here also.

Some back stories are told here for the first time though, and some people in them have not been prominently or publicly identified before. For several of them, their names and nicknames have been changed and their identities obscured for various reasons.

Because this story takes place in a law firm, to protect clients' privacy and confidentiality the identities of cases and clients and have been disguised by changing case names and facts. Some attorneys' names have been changed also. The tedium, stress, and personal interactions involved are portrayed realistically. In a few instances, the timing of incidents has been compressed or modified slightly in the interest of making a long story a little shorter.

Finally, while parts of this book reflect the frustration, discouragement, and insecurity of a young attorney's work, I would like to emphasize that I believe Latham & Watkins to be one of the finest law firms in the world. Nothing I say here is intended to criticize Latham specifically. It was simply the nature of big firm law practice that didn't agree with me. But they paid me well for it.

It was Latham, after all, that took on Mario's case when no one else would, invested millions of dollars in attorney time and expenses in it, and stayed with it for eight years, even when at times it looked hopeless. The case didn't earn Latham a cent, but it changed my life.

Ian Graham
Santa Monica, California
October 2009

UNBILLABLE HOURS

A TRUE STORY

CHAPTER 1

I'm Going to Prison

CALIPATRIA STATE PRISON, AUGUST 2005

THREADING MY WAY east along the 10 Freeway toward downtown Los Angeles early on a Wednesday morning, I knew what was waiting in my office. A senior partner on the forty-fourth floor was expecting a draft of a demurrer motion I'd promised him by midday. Another partner, on forty-two, wanted to talk to me "urgently" about a new insurance defense case he was staffing. I had interrogatories to answer in an employment case and deposition prep to do for a toxic tort case that was starting on Monday. But approaching downtown, I didn't take the Sixth Street exit, which led to the associates' parking garage across from my office building. Instead, I stayed straight on the 10, heading east toward Palm Springs and beyond, my knuckles frozen white on the wheel.

In the passenger seat next to me the papers were stacked a foot high, a constant reminder of what lay ahead. I couldn't stop glancing over, wishing I'd put them out of sight—as if that would have made a difference. With each glance, my throat tightened and my right foot pressed down a little harder on the accelerator, pushing my new Range Rover past ninety on the California interstate.

I was on my way to the maximum-security Calipatria State Prison to deliver a coded note from a person on the outside, a veteran of the California prison system with influence inside the walls, clearing my client, Mario Rocha, of blame for something I had written. The handwritten note, concealed among hundreds of pages of meaningless legal cases, was serious contraband. If I got caught with it, I could be arrested and probably disbarred. I could lose my job, my career, and my new house in Santa Monica.

And Mario could be murdered in prison in a matter of days.

Even if I succeeded today, Mario would spend the rest of his life in prison unless I could get his conviction overturned. At the age of sixteen, he had been convicted as an adult for a murder he had not committed. He was serving a double life sentence with no possibility of parole. At twenty-five, a couple of years younger than me, Mario had been in prison for nine years. Overturning his conviction was, at best, a ten-thousand-to-one long shot.

Why am I doing this? I thought. *This is way outside my job description.* As a fourth-year associate at the ultra-white-shoe law firm of Latham & Watkins, I spent most of my time grinding out motions and memos for Fortune 500 companies, movie studios, and professional sports franchises in mega-million-dollar litigation. And while the firm encouraged associates like me to work on unpaid pro bono cases as a way to get hands-on legal experience and serve the community, my mission today was not exactly what the firm had in mind. Latham had recently warned me that my billable hours were low compared with those of other associates and that failure to fix this "would negatively affect my future at the firm."

For a few miles, I began to panic. *I should turn around. I should go back to the office. I should get my billable work done.*

Somewhere past Palm Springs, with the Salton Sea shimmering in the distance, I was finally able to start putting my thoughts together. I had focused blindly on winning, my way, in the latest habeas corpus petition I had filed for Mario. Believing I had found a legal silver bullet, I'd made a big—and very possibly fatal—mistake.

I had cited evidence I'd recently discovered in police files that another teenager from LA's Latino barrio, a gang member called "Joker," might have done the crime instead of Mario. And I had ignored the inmates' unbreakable code of silence.

In my last visit to Calipatria, Mario had warned me about what could happen if I pointed a finger at Joker. "He's in here with me," Mario had whispered, "and you can't bring his name into this, he's *connected.*"

But I had pressed Mario about the police report implicating Joker. This might be our last chance to get him a new trial, and this was important information. I promised to emphasize that I'd found the evidence pointing to Joker in public police files, and that it had not come from Mario. I argued that no one inside the prison except Mario would ever see my petition. All Mario would say was, "I'm not saying anything more about this."

On my own, I had described the police report in a footnote

and added that it had come from a public source. I was a young lawyer, zealously representing my client, as the Canons of Legal Ethics say an attorney should. But I didn't know prisons. In a maximum-security prison there are no secrets among inmates and no exceptions to their code. Snitching—informing on another inmate—is a cardinal sin. Snitches are killed. Through the invisible web of the prison system, other inmates had seen the petition and word had spread on the prison grapevine that Mario had snitched.

Twice, Mario had been attacked, stabbed, and nearly killed. The next attack would likely be fatal. And it was my fault.

I'd asked the prison to put Mario into protective custody, but Mario had refused. "Protective custody is for snitches and child molesters," he scolded me. In tense, roundabout whispers over the phone, I learned what had to be done: I had to present evidence to a person on the outside who had influence among the Mexican inmates inside the prison that Mario had not snitched and that I had found and used the evidence against Joker on my own.

For a week, I worked as usual from nine to nine on billable law firm business. And then I went home and worked into the morning hours drafting a long letter to a person I didn't know, the veteran of the California prison system with connections on the inside, showing that Mario had not snitched and that the evidence pointing to Joker had come from public police files. I attached to my letter a copy of the police report that had identified Joker, along with the transcript of every statement Mario had made to the police. Through go-betweens, my letter and attachments found their way to the right person.

A week later, a response made its way back to me in the form of a handwritten note, called a "kite," or "wila" in prison slang. In Spanish, and in code that its addressees would understand, the note said that Mario had not snitched and that the attacks against him were unjustified.

I had assumed that one of Mario's family members would deliver the note to him. But family visits weren't allowed until the following weekend and this couldn't wait. Besides, I was told, guards monitor family visits more closely than those of attorneys. So it fell to me to get the note to Mario without getting arrested, disbarred, and disgraced. This wasn't about billing hours. It was about saving a life.

CALIPATRIA, A RAMSHACKLE town of seven thousand in the El Centro Desert, near the spot where the state lines of California and Arizona touch the border of Mexico, is desolate by any standard. It is in one of the poorest counties in California. The leading businesses are a pesticide plant, a slaughterhouse, and the super-max prison. An acrid smell of rotten milk hangs over the whole area. Calipatria's main claim to fame is that it is the lowest-lying city in the Western Hemisphere; besides the prison, its chief attraction is a 184-foot flagpole whose top reaches sea level. The prison packs in 4,200 inmates, twice its design capacity. It's the place where Angelo Buono, "the Hillside Strangler," was found dead in his cell in 2002.

I spotted the guard tower first, tall and ominous in the distance. Soon a high chain-link fence, topped with concertina wire, ran parallel along the highway on my left. It was almost 11:00 A.M. by the time I slowed my car to a crawl, took a deep breath, and turned left into the prison's main entrance. A newly tarred asphalt road led to the visitor and staff parking lot. I parked next to a big black pickup truck, its body lifted high above the wheels, with a bumper sticker that read, KILL 'EM ALL, LET GOD SORT 'EM OUT. The truck belonged, I presumed, to one of the prison guards.

It was at least 110 degrees. I could feel the hot asphalt through my shoes as I walked across the parking lot to the building where visitors checked in, lugging my stack of papers in my big litigation briefcase. A blast of cool air hit me as I walked inside. The guard at the desk wasn't busy, but he ignored me as long as he could, a not-so-subtle statement that I was on his turf.

"You're here for Rocha?" he finally asked.

I nodded, forcing a smile.

"You been here before?"

I nodded again.

Familiar with the drill, I placed my bar card and driver's license on the counter, deposited my watch, keys, and cell phone in a small locker against the wall, and stood with my arms out as the guard waved a metal detector over me.

"What's in the case?" he asked.

"Just some legal papers—cases and notes" I replied too quickly, opening the top of the briefcase to show him.

Then he handed me the standard form that visitors sign. In large print, it said that, by signing it, I was swearing that I was not bringing into the prison any contraband, including "any gang-related writings, drawings or other unauthorized communications." I stared at those words for a long moment, forgetting that the guard was watching and that my hesitation might look suspicious. At last I signed in a shaky hand. I was now committed irrevocably.

A massive guard with an angry scowl, a large sidearm, and a billy club that looked as though it had seen its fair share of action, unlocked a door at the rear of the room and waved me through. The door led to a small outdoor area, enclosed by a chain-link fence, between the reception building and the prison's outer wall. I stood there facing the massive steel door that led through the thick stone wall. After a few seconds, a buzzer sounded and the door slowly slid open and then closed with a clank behind me. I found myself standing on the long road that encircles the prison. A scowling guard sat facing me in a golf cart, its roof shading him from the sun.

"See that big red *D* outside those doors down there?" he said, nodding toward a building at least a hundred yards down the road. "That's where you're headed. I'll meet you there."

With that, he sped off in his cart, leaving me to walk the length of a football field carrying my briefcase in the 110-degree heat. I walked slowly. It was too hot to move any other way.

My shirt was soaked through by the time I reached the doors to Building D, where the guard sat waiting in the shade of his cart. Silently, he unlocked the doors and led me into the visiting room and then to a seat in front of a small cubicle. I sat down facing a wire-reinforced glass partition between me and an empty chair on the other side.

"Wait here," the guard commanded as he took a seat against the wall twenty feet away.

It's amazing how long five minutes can seem. The air-conditioning hissed to a halt and sweat dripped from my forehead as

I pulled the stack of papers out of my briefcase. I placed them on the counter in front of me, looking quickly to make sure the note was still concealed, and then stared through the glass at the empty chair.

At last Mario appeared on the other side of the partition, shackled at his wrists and ankles, shuffling across the floor in a dark blue prison jumpsuit. He looked thin compared to his usually broad, prison-lean, and buffed frame. As he sat down, a guard on his side of the partition unlocked his handcuffs and disappeared from sight.

Mario and I picked up the phones on either side of the glass and tried to make small talk. It was beyond awkward. We both knew the only reason I was there was to pass him the note, but we had to make this look like a regular attorney visit.

"How are you doing?" I stammered, feeling ridiculous at asking the question: he was in the prison infirmary after having been almost stabbed to death.

"Good. I'm good," Mario replied, equally absurdly. "You wanna see the scars?"

Not really.

But I nodded, since we had to talk about something. Mario stood up and lifted his shirt. Big, ugly, red scars crossed his abdomen and punctuated his chest. He pointed to the front and back of his shoulder, where the blade had gone clear through. For an instant I was embarrassed, sitting in a prison staring at a man's bare torso, but those scars also shocked me back to the realization of why I was there. Mario could have been dead, and he soon might be unless we pulled this off.

After twenty more minutes spent talking in generalities

about his case, it was time. I stood up, turned to the guard, and told him we were done but that I had some legal papers to pass to Mario. The guard walked over, still scowling. I handed him the stack of pages containing the contraband note.

"Any staples or paper clips?"

"No. It's just some cases with some notes I made."

My heart was pounding so hard I had trouble keeping my balance as the guard began flipping through the pages. He was looking too closely. Not page by page, but close enough to find the note. I felt my face flush and looked away, pretending to scratch my shoulder with my chin so he couldn't see the naked fear on my face.

As he reached the last third of the pages—exactly where the note was hidden—he paused.

"What's this?"

CHAPTER 2

Make Me an Offer

SIX YEARS EARLIER,
AUSTIN, TEXAS, SEPTEMBER 1999

"SO TELL ME why you want to be a lawyer?" asked the pale, heavy-set law firm partner sitting across the desk from me.

I don't, really. I'm here for the summer job I heard about where you pay me $2,500 a week to eat shrimp cocktail and drink beer.

That would have been the truth. Fortunately, the law school career services office had provided me with a better response to such a question, filled with all the right buzzwords, as a kind of survival guide for interviewees. So I told the pasty lawyer something about my passion for the law, with all its intellectual challenges, mental stimulation, and competition: just what I wanted in my career. Hearing myself speak, I felt like an ass. I didn't believe any of it. This guy probably heard the same line from everyone he interviewed. He couldn't really be buying this crap, could he?

But as I finished, the partner was smiling and nodding his

head in agreement. "That's great, Ian. I think that's exactly right," he said. You've got to have a passion for the intellectual side of the job. Otherwise, we'd all just be doing it for the money."

"Um, right."

It was the first week of my second year of law school at the University of Texas, a period known as the fall recruiting season, when partners from the top law firms all over the country swarmed to the Austin campus—and those of other law schools—to interview second-year law students whose first-year grades had met their standards. They were there to recruit us to be summer associates with them for the following summer, during which time they would try to persuade us to accept their offers of full-time jobs at hefty six-figure salaries, to start after we finished our third and final year of law school.

It was a seller's market. In the booming economy of the late nineties, law firms were expanding fast and needed young associates to cover their ever increasing work demands. The biggest and most prestigious firms prided themselves on recruiting only the top students from the top-tier law schools. Competition for these recruits had driven those firms to pay their summer associates as much as $2,500 a week, to drop all pretense of requiring much work from them, and to concentrate instead on treating them to fancy lunches, social events, and fine dinners at partners' homes and country clubs. Most law students, even those who didn't necessarily want to work for a firm, were chasing these jobs at the biggest, highest-paying firms.

That was me. I wasn't sure what I wanted to do after law school. I never thought I'd actually want to *be* a lawyer. Growing up in Washington, D.C., and attending Sidwell Friends, a private Quaker prep school catering to the children of A-list Democrats, including the daughters of Presidents Clinton and Obama, I'd always been surrounded by lawyers; almost every kid I knew had at least one lawyer parent. But it had never seemed like a particularly exciting job. To me, lawyers wore dark suits, worked very hard, and for affluent people, they didn't seem very happy. My father was a lawyer, a partner in a large firm, and even though he was at the top of his profession, he worked long hours, on weekends, and while on vacation. I'd heard his stories of the constant pressure, the client demands, and the big-firm politics. He didn't love it. I suspect he didn't even like it. And he always dropped a lot of suggestions that I should *not* be a lawyer. Actually, what he'd say was, "I'm doing this shit so you and your sister won't have to."

What I *wanted* to do, what I was sure I was going to do, was be a baseball player. And while a baseball scholarship to Rice University prolonged my delusion somewhat, by my sophomore year it was pretty clear that pro baseball wasn't going to be an option for a 5′10″, 160-pound utility infielder with "a bat like wet newspaper," as my coach described my swing. Still, even if baseball wasn't my future, I enjoyed being part of a top-ranked team and playing alongside five future Major Leaguers. But with four hours of practice six days a week in the fall and a seventy-game schedule in the spring, I didn't have much time or inclination for long-term career planning.

Before I knew it, I was wearing a cap and gown, sitting on a folding chair in the Rice quad, and listening to Kurt Vonnegut tell me I probably wasn't going to amount to much, but that was okay. Now, Vonnegut was, and still is, one of my favorite authors, but it occurred to me that a man who made his living writing offbeat doomsday science fiction might have some trouble offering perspective to eager young people about to enter the real world. After warning us that we were a race of "planet gobblers" who, if left unchecked, were on a course to destroy the earth, Vonnegut offered some career advice: aim low. According to Kurt, we couldn't all be Kurt. Most of us would find that our ambition to do great things or to lead remarkable lives would only result in misery and failure. We should find a job we could do, do it well, and happily accept a pat on the back and a "job well done" as our reward. Good motherly advice. But I wasn't having it. I was twenty-two and precocious. I was going to do something exciting, something I was passionate about—and make bags of money doing it. Exactly what that was, however, I wasn't sure.

For lack of anything better, after graduating from Rice I slumped back home to Washington and found a job as the lowliest staffer for the House Ways and Means Committee, and waited for inspiration to strike. For the next six months, I sat at a desk behind an unmarked door in the Longworth Building, on Capitol Hill, answering questions and absorbing abuse from irate taxpayers, at a salary slightly above minimum wage.

My friends had bigger plans. Some were heading to Wall Street firms to make piles of money, or to business school and then to Wall Street. Others were going to law school or medical school. One had been accepted to Columbia Law School but had deferred enrollment in order to take a six-figure job at Goldman Sachs. That was about standard. As a "dipshit Ways and Means lackey" (one frequent caller's characterization of me), I felt as though I was falling behind, that my friends' careers were taking on higher trajectories than mine. And I began to stew. As a math-and-science-phobic government major, I had neither the preparation nor the knack for Wall Street or medical school. But law school I figured I could do. And although I didn't necessarily want to be a lawyer, I thought law school would give me three more years to do some of the thinking I had not done in college, and a law degree would be a nice credential.

In other words, I went to law school for the same reason a lot of people do: because I got in and because I didn't know what else to do.

"If you are here because you didn't know what else to do, then you are here for the wrong reason." These were the first words in the dean's opening remarks to my first-year law school class.

Apparently, this was a common problem. Most law students, said the dean, are type-A personalities who don't take well to being in the middle of a pack. Rudderless law students, he warned, would find themselves victims of their own ambition.

"The primitive brain will take over if you let it," he continued.

The best grades get you onto law review? I wanna be on law review. The best firms interview only the top students? I wanna interview with the best firms.

"It becomes a herd mentality," he said, "and you can get swept up in it."

And from there, the primrose path narrows: from first-year grades to interviews with fancy law firms, to cushy summer jobs, to a career in big-firm law practice, so that we—the undecided but ambitious—soon find ourselves living a life we perhaps did not expect but could not resist.

"If that describes you, then mark my words," the dean concluded, "the trade-offs will show up later."

I had no history of competing academically. I was lucky to have gotten into law school at all. And my innocence protected me. My classmates, I figured, were the ones who would be competing for the best grades and best jobs. My goal going into it was simply not to embarrass myself.

The first year of law school is a shock to most who come straight from college. The Socratic method of teaching used on first-years, where the professor picks out a hapless student at the beginning of class and grills him at length in front of his peers, is an instant immersion in learning to "think like a lawyer," on your feet and under pressure—the equivalent of medical school's early exposure of its students to blood and gore. Most law students tend to be former hotshot undergraduates, and a lot of law professors, like marine drill instructors, take pleasure in knocking them down before building them up. "From time to time it may be necessary for me to point out the extent of your stupidity," one of my professors told us with a smile.

So I kept up, reading and briefing cases and learning to spot legal issues. Maybe because (at first) I didn't think I was gunning for the best grades, the law review, or a big-firm job, I didn't feel the pressure that seemed to afflict so many of my classmates. And without that added stress, midway through the first semester I began to feel comfortable enough to think that with a little luck on the exams I could finish the year in the top half of my class.

When our first-semester grades were posted, I was surprised to see that I was near the top.

That's when my head started to turn. In one semester, my history of academic mediocrity had been erased and, *poof,* replaced with a grade point average that said I was no longer Ian Graham, lucky-to-be-here law student, but Ian Graham, top law student.

I worked even harder in the spring semester, and did even better.

Now, in the fall of my second year, though I hadn't thought I wanted to work at a big firm, a summer job for $2,500 a week didn't sound so bad, and the prospect of a six-figure income after graduation was starting to sound pretty nice, too. And with my first-year grades, the firms my classmates were begging to be interviewed by were begging to interview me. Just as the dean had warned, I got caught up in the frenzy.

Every morning during fall recruiting, before we embarked on our daily series of twenty-minute interviews, the lobby of the Career Services Building was packed with nervous law students in their "interview" suits, holding folders containing their résumés and transcripts and exchanging gossip about law firms. *That firm is a sweatshop. I have a friend who knows somebody who works there, and she billed three thousand hours last year.* Or, *I heard that firm has the best summer program, and they're bumping up first-year salaries next year.* I tried to ignore most of the chatter, but it was comforting to hear that many of my classmates' motives were as shallow as mine. The gossip was always about two things: billable hours and money.

These on-campus interviews were the first step in a mating

game to determine who would receive callbacks—invitations to fly to a firm's home city for a day of getting-to-know-you interviews. They were like quick first dates, including the need sometimes to hold one's tongue and imagine.

"Why do you want to practice law?" *(I don't, really. I just want to get paid well for a fun summer job.)*

"Why do you want to work for this firm?" *(I hardly know anything about this firm, other than I've heard of it and it pays well.)*

"Why are you interested in working in Los Angeles/D.C./New York?" *(Because it seems like a good place to spend the summer.)*

I kept waiting for all this to come to a screeching halt. Considering what these firms were offering—big pay for an easy summer job with an almost guaranteed offer to join the firm for even bigger pay after graduation—surely they would dig a little deeper than just my résumé and one year of law school grades. At any moment I feared one of the interviewers would wave my undergraduate transcript in my face and ask me to explain how, as a Division-I baseball player, I had gotten a C-minus in Coaching Baseball, or had failed an introductory political science course nicknamed Bombs and Rockets. But this never happened. And the doors were opening fast.

At one interview, a partner from the Austin office of a large national firm eagerly shot out of his chair as I entered the room and shook my hand enthusiastically. "Ah bet you know James Dole?" he drawled with a smile, referring to James Doyle, the father of one of my Rice teammates, who was a well-known Houston lawyer and a big Rice baseball supporter. I answered that I did. "Well, then, unless yew bite a pardner's wife in the ass tonight, yer hired!" he said, slapping me on the back. The "tonight" he was referring to was a cocktail party his firm was hosting at a local bar for interviewees they liked. That was it. I hadn't even sat down. I'd aced the shortest interview in law school history.

And then there was Latham & Watkins. The firm had started in an LA storefront during the Depression and now had more than two thousand attorneys in twenty-four countries, partners who drew seven-figure incomes, and a global Fortune 500 client list. Latham had recently been named "Law Firm of the Decade" by a prominent international panel, and had been near the top of the *American Lawyer*'s "A-List" every year since the rankings began. It was a place where worried CEOs took their bet-the-business litigation and their billion-dollar deals. Among the big firms interviewing on campus, Latham also had a reputation around the law school as a younger, hipper firm than its peers. And it was also widely thought that it had the most lavish and raucous summer program. One of my more uptight classmates told me she had passed on Latham's offer to interview her because of the firm's "fratlike atmosphere," where "everybody just goes out and gets drunk." Which sounded to me like a point in the firm's favor.

The afternoon before my Latham interview, John Dalton, a silver-haired, tanned senior partner in the firm's Orange County office, hosted a cocktail party for all interviewees at the Hula Hut, a popular Austin bar. Dressed in a Hawaiian shirt, shorts, and flip-flops, he announced, "No pressure today. Just have a few margaritas and enjoy yourselves. I'll be here if you have any questions." He looked relaxed, rich, and satisfied—all the things I wanted to be.

My interview the next day started with a warm greeting: "I've been waiting for this one. I like your style," Dalton said. I wasn't sure what he meant, but...whatever; it was a good start. He made sure to hit all the key interview points—why I was going to law school, why Latham, why LA—but there was none of the awkwardness or formality there had been in some other interviews. (At one of these, a partner from a D.C. firm introduced himself, shook my hand, and then pulled out a bottle of hand sanitizer and disinfected himself.) It felt like a casual conversation. We talked about life in Southern California, sports, politics. He waxed about Latham. It was a "slice of heaven" for him. He worked on cutting-edge legal issues and was surrounded by brilliant people. The firm atmosphere was "open and friendly." Latham, he said, "is the big firm that doesn't act like a big firm," a claim I would hear many times during the recruiting process, along with "I wouldn't practice law anywhere else." When our twenty minutes were up, things had apparently gone well. Dalton invited me to join him and a few other interviewees he felt were "Latham people" for dinner that night at Sullivan's, one of Austin's best restaurants.

I can't begin to guess what the dinner bill came to that night. For three hours, nine of us—Dalton, seven of my classmates, and I—drank countless bottles of fine wine and ate the best surf and turf in the city as we listened to all the great things Dalton said about Latham. When I finally excused myself, fearing I wouldn't be able to stand up if I stayed any longer, Dalton pulled me aside. "I really hope you come out for a callback with us, Ian. I'm going to put in a good word for you. You're a Latham guy. I can feel it."

I was beginning to feel it, too.

I received five callback offers, from firms in LA, New York, and Washington, all of whom wanted to fly me out for a full day of follow-up interviews at their offices, put me up in four-star hotel suites, and, if things went well, wine and dine me. It had been only a year since I'd wandered into law school. This was heady stuff.

Some of the callback interviews were off-putting, and others were flat-out strange. At a prestigious international firm in LA, most of the attorneys I was scheduled to meet with were too busy or couldn't be bothered to see me. So I was bounced around to substitute interviewers, who seemed annoyed they had to spend twenty minutes talking to me. The only partner I met spent the first fifteen minutes of our twenty-minute session talking on the phone to a buddy about a recent golf trip to Scotland, all the time winking and nodding at me as though I were in on the conversation. When he finally hung up, he said, "It feels good to be king. You got any more questions?"

At a big firm in Washington, an intense young litigation partner began our interview by leaning back in his chair with his feet on the desk and silently eyeballing me for several minutes while he gnawed on, and then appeared to actually eat, what looked like a wooden coffee stirrer. "I see you're not on law review," he finally said. "Don't you consider yourself a *winner*? We only hire winners here." His voice began to rise. "I don't *ever* fucking lose...*neeeverrrrr*!"

Again, Latham stood out. The office was located in the seventy-four-story, stone-and-steel I. M. Pei–designed U.S. Bank Tower, the tallest building west of the Mississippi, at the center of the high-rent Bunker Hill district in downtown LA. The polished marble lobby was filled with well-dressed people coming and going. A high-speed elevator with a television showing news and stock quotes shot me to the main Latham reception area on the fortieth floor, where Joy, Latham's stunning, blond, midtwenties hiring coordinator, greeted me with a smile. She handed me a schedule for the day and gave me a quick tour.

Latham's LA office, which served as the firm's worldwide headquarters, occupied the sixth and the thirty-fifth through forty-fifth floors of the building. The structure's round design left no place for corner offices, slightly muting the subtle but clear pecking order. Among the attorneys' offices ringing the outer walls, partners' offices were bigger and had the best views. Secretaries' bays and paralegal and staff offices sat on the inside of the building, separated from those of the attorneys by a carpeted hallway encircling each floor. On the walls were large original photographs, each floor with a different theme: famous architecture on thirty-eight, iconic portraits on forty-two. There was a large law library staffed with full-time librarians on forty-one, and on the sixth floor, an attorney dining room where breakfast was free and lunch was only six dollars.

Also on six were the conference rooms where Latham attorneys faced off against opposing parties like Samurai warriors. The photographs surrounding the conference rooms on six were a not-so-subtle statement to outsiders: a lion mauling a gazelle, a bull trampling a runner in Pamplona, a tank crushing a bicycle.

"Everything is set up so that attorneys can focus on their work," Joy told me. Almost an entire floor was devoted to a Document Support Center, where attorneys could drop off marked-up drafts at any hour of any day or night and get them back within hours as edited, finished documents. On floor thirty-eight there was an Operations Center with round-the-clock secretarial, paralegal, and technical support and the ability to handle any attorney request, from dinner orders to car service to travel arrangements (although Latham had an in-house travel agency, too).

The interviews at Latham that day were crisp, and the day went by quickly. Compared to some attorneys I had met at other firms, those at Latham all seemed like surprisingly normal people. They were pleasant and upbeat. The partners all expressed pride in the firm. "This is the big leagues," one of them said. "I would never practice anywhere else." They emphasized that Latham gave young attorneys training and responsibility early in their careers and that every associate had a chance to make partner. "You're not going to get stuck reviewing documents for two years here," they told me.

"Latham," each and every one of them said, "is the big firm that doesn't act like a big firm."

The associates were also friendly and positive about the firm. They acknowledged that they were busy and that there were occasional periods of long hours, but they said the work "ebbed and flowed." They emphasized that associates got meaningful work and hands-on experience early in their careers. The requirement of 1,900 billable hours a year wasn't so bad, they said, and they raved about Latham's summer program, saying it was by far the most fun and lavish in LA and a great way to get to know the city and the firm.

At the end of the day, Jim Arnold, a partner on Latham's

Recruiting Committee, met me in the lobby with a big smile. He shook my hand and offered me a summer associate job on the spot. Actually, he said the firm would be "honored if you would join us next summer." I thought the interviews had gone well, but most firms took weeks or months after callback interviews to extend offers. I tried to play it cool and muttered something about being flattered but still having other firms to visit. But before I could finish, he slapped me on the back and introduced me to two senior associates he said were taking me to dinner at Spago in Beverly Hills to celebrate.

I tried to hold out. I did have more interviews scheduled. But the associates with me at Spago were a lot of fun and very persuasive. For three hours, as we made our way through four courses and three bottles of wine, we talked about life at Latham. They told me they loved working at Latham and couldn't imagine going anywhere else. And they said the Latham summer program was by far the best of any firm. "Dude, you'll have a blast out here. Guaranteed. Just say yes, and we order the Dom Pérignon."

The offer was hard to resist, and I wasn't sure I wanted to. A little over a year earlier, I'd been in a crowded cubicle answering phone calls from angry taxpayers, clueless about what to do next. In Austin, I lived in a small studio apartment with an inflatable couch. Now I was being wined and dined by senior associates from one of the most prestigious law firms in the country and having my arm twisted to accept $2,500 a week to be recruited during a pleasant summer. At the end of the evening, I accepted Latham's offer to be a summer associate at the end of my second year of law school.

And so I found myself, on a Friday evening in the fall of my second year in law school, on a sidewalk outside one of Beverly Hills's finest restaurants, my head pleasantly buzzing with wine, and a summer job and possible career at Latham & Watkins in my pocket.

I tried to keep some perspective. "We'll see," I told myself. "Maybe I'll like it, maybe I won't." Either way, I was going to be spending a well-paid summer in LA.

IF THERE EVER was a job I was suited for, it was big-firm summer associate.

Shortly before leaving Austin for LA, I received an unexpected $2,500 check for "relocation expenses." The envelope also held a facebook of my fellow "summers." It appeared I was in good company: twenty-eight men and seventeen women from law schools such as Harvard, Yale, Stanford, Chicago, UCLA, Berkeley, and Michigan, all looking bright and eager.

The first morning of the summer, Jim Arnold greeted us in the fortieth-floor reception area. He knew all forty-five of us by name and was smooth and funny as he told us what to expect. He said with a smile that we should *try* to bill a few hours a day and, at some point over the next twelve weeks, produce at least one piece of written work that the Recruiting Committee could evaluate. But it was clear that this was pretty much a formality. We would come to understand that work was only a small part of the summer experience. Getting to know the attorneys and fellow summers through social events was at least equally important. We would be taken to lunch almost every day by associates and partners, there would be dinners out or other events two or three times a week, and we would be invited to private homes for dinners and cocktail parties. (The dinners, which were usually held at the elegant homes of senior partners, were known to associates as TCBY, or "This Could Be Yours," events.) Latham's luxury box at Dodger Stadium was ours to use as we pleased. There would be two weekend trips, one to a resort in San Diego over the coming weekend and the other for white-water rafting near the end of the summer. Arnold closed by telling us we were to leave at two o'clock that afternoon to attend a taping of *The Tonight Show* with Jay Leno at NBC studios in Burbank. With that, we were shown to our offices, where our names were inscribed on big silver plates beside our doors, and introduced to our secretaries.

I got to know the other summers quickly. Mostly, it was a great group, with the expected range of backgrounds and personalities. Some were serious and bookish, some loud and funny, some a little too overtly competitive— "There's an A-team and a B-team here. You wanna get with the A-team," one of the summers told me during the first week. But unlike in law school, we weren't competing against one another: Latham had made it clear that it hoped to give all of us offers at the end of the summer. At one or two meetings we were basically told, "Welcome to Latham. Have a good time!"

And we did. On the first weekend we gathered at a four-star resort in San Diego, along with the summers from all of Latham's U.S. offices, for Latham's "Summer Academy." There were beach volleyball and water polo games against the other offices, decadent dinners, a Las Vegas–themed casino party, and a hospitality suite stocked with booze that turned into a nerdy version of *Animal House* every night. As I entered the suite on Friday night, Brian Gordon, up to this point a quiet kid from Harvard Law, was in the corner singing Elvis songs at the top of his lungs as he alternated swigs from the bottle of red wine in his right hand and bottle of white in his left. Chris Lee, from Boalt (UC Berkeley), had just finished a beer bong and was throwing up into a potted plant. On the patio other summers were chugging beers and tossing the empty bottles over their heads without looking, where they smashed onto the concrete pool deck close to terrified hotel guests. And it wasn't just summers. Associates and partners were in there, too, getting drunk and high-fiving summer associates. Jim Arnold did a beer bong. I held it for him.

I became good friends with three summers in particular: Matt Barnes, a hedonist from Harvard Law who spent almost every night of the summer at the bars and clubs in Hollywood, lugging with him a beer bong with LA RULES printed on the side; Trevor Wilson, a quick-witted local from UCLA Law whose office was next to mine on the forty-second floor; and Mike Wilke, a former pro baseball catcher, now at Georgetown Law, who was built like a tank and spoke with a Long Island accent. We went out almost every night and even took a few trips to Las Vegas to put our fancy paychecks to work.

The work that summer was easy, or "about as challenging as getting to the bottom of a waterslide," as Trevor put it. Mostly I accompanied partners to meetings with clients and to hearings in court. Now and then I was asked to analyze a few cases and write a memo, but there were never tight deadlines, and the partners and associates were always approachable for questions.

At one point, when a few of us had been asked to do some research that kept us at the office late one night, the partner in charge of the case came by the next morning, apologized profusely, and offered to take us to lunch.

At the end of the summer, despite numerous displays of drunken inappropriateness and little attention to work, forty-four of the forty-five summer associates in Latham's LA office, including Matt, Trevor, Mike, and me, received offers to join Latham as associate attorneys after our third year of law school.

I took a few months to make up my mind about the offer, but there was never really any question. I knew the past summer had been mostly about recruiting and that real law practice would be very different. Latham had tried to hide it, but I had noticed a few associates walking around with their eyes bloodshot and dressed in the same clothes they had on the day before. I knew I would be working long hours. But it was hard to get that summer out of my head and to conjure up a realistic sense of how different real law practice would be.

I looked for alternatives, but not very hard. I interviewed with a few sports agencies and with a sports media company in New York. They all required new hires to start in the mail room for eight dollars an hour, even if they had law degrees. Latham was offering a base salary of $125,000 a year plus a bonus, based on billable hours, of up to $50,000. For that amount, their requirement of 1,900 billable hours a year didn't seem bad. Besides, I had made friends at Latham and had had a great time over the summer. Latham just seemed like my kind of place.

Shortly before Thanksgiving, I accepted Latham's offer.

At a wedding that fall of one of my good high-school friends, some of the parents who were lawyers congratulated me with an undertone of surprise: "Ian, I *always knew* you had it in you." Bridesmaids' mothers tried to set me up with their daughters. In the world where I had grown up, a job at Latham was a stamp of validation, a sign, as my friend's new bride put it when she thought I wasn't listening, that "Ian finally has his shit together."

If I'd had a little more will power, I might have stepped back and asked why one the biggest and best law firms in the world had to recruit so hard. I would have asked how a firm that hires some fifty new law school graduates for its LA office, but makes only one or two of them partners eight or more years later, could expect incoming associates to believe that all new hires had a shot at partnership. I would have thought carefully about the rumors around law school that all big firms, no matter what they say, are sweatshops for young associates. I would have thought about the fact that I'd seen only the well-crafted glimpse of the firm that Latham had wanted me to see.

—ꟺ—

CHAPTER 3

Welcome Back

RESTON, VIRGINIA, OCTOBER 2001

STANDING IN A grassy field in Virginia trying to coax a large Russian man to hold my hand is not how I'd expected to start my career as an associate at Latham.

According to his name tag, he is Igor from the Moscow office. He is built like a heavyweight Greco-Roman wrestler, and judging from the look on his face, he would rather pull my arm off and beat me to death with it than hold my hand. I'm not thrilled about it, either, but the entire class of worldwide incoming Latham associates—more than 250—is standing in a "friendship circle" already holding hands. Igor and I are the only break in the chain.

I extend my hand and try to entice him: "C'mon, big fella, paws up." No reaction. I try humor: "Hey, at least it can't get any more awkward than this!" Igor doesn't budge. Others in the circle are starting to whisper, or at least I think they are. After a few tense moments, from somewhere in our circle I hear a woman's voice bark something in Russian. And finally, with a look of disdain and humiliation on his face, Igor grabs my wrist, and our Latham friendship circle is complete.

The friendship circle was the final activity of a weekend-long orientation at what the firm called Latham & Watkins University, or LWU. All of Latham's incoming associates were called "stubs" because, after spending the summer studying for and then taking the bar exam (at Latham's expense), we were starting late in the year and only had a stub of a billable year left. We would become fully fledged first-year associates on January 1.

For the orientation, we were sequestered in a Marriott in Reston, Virginia, a lifeless corporate town near Dulles Airport, to learn how the firm operated, where we fit in, and what was expected of us. The day after LWU weekend, I would start my legal career in earnest.

From the beginning of the weekend, it was painfully clear that recruiting was over. LWU was the coyote morning to the weekend boondoggle at the four-star retreat in San Diego that had kicked off the previous summer. At LWU there was no beach volleyball or water polo, no Latham T-shirts or coffee mugs, no partners high-fiving associates, and no hospitality suite with free booze flowing all night. It was three days of tightly scheduled seminars with mandatory attendance and monitored sign-in sheets.

Already, the buzz at LWU was not good: layoffs. It had been more than a year since my summer at Latham, and in the intervening time a lot had happened to put law firms and the country on edge. The tech boom that had sprouted dot-com companies out of every garage in Silicon Valley—and created armies of paper millionaires in need of legal advice—had faltered, causing the national economy to slide into a recession and an entire market for legal services to almost vanish. Law firms like Latham that had hired large numbers of associates to meet the work demands of the dot-com boom were now overstaffed and reeling. The hottest law firm in the country in recent years—Brobeck, Phleger & Harrison, of San Francisco and Silicon Valley—had collapsed over the summer, putting hundreds of that firm's high-powered partners and associates on the stagnant California job market. Rumors were swirling that more big California law firms, including Latham, would be cutting back soon.

September 11—*that* 9/11—had happened a month earlier. The stock market had lost more than $3 trillion in value and an economy already in recession had tanked. No one knew what would happen next.

The first evening of LWU, we eagerly filled every seat of the hotel's largest ballroom to hear Tom Baylor, Latham's managing partner, reassure us in his welcome-to-the-firm address that our paychecks were safe. But Baylor spent most of his talk enthusiastically telling us about the recent opening of Latham's Hamburg office, "our third office in Germany!" I wasn't sure why he thought anyone cared about this, until I spotted a clutch of twenty or so German lawyers sitting near the front of the room beaming with pride at their recognition. Finally, Baylor segued to how Latham's aggressive growth, expansion, and diversification had positioned the firm not only to survive the tough economic times, but to *thrive.* Our size and breadth of expertise enabled us to handle the most complex local, national, and international business deals and litigation, and to do it faster, better, and more efficiently than our competitors. These huge, geographically far-flung, multiple-moving-part deals and litigations—requiring the specialized expertise of dozens of partners, each billing between $500 and $1,000 per hour, backstopped by hundreds of associates billing from $200 to $400 an hour and working round the clock for years on end—were Latham's bread and butter.

Our clients were brand-name companies and others who, though Baylor didn't say it this way, could afford our rates. We didn't represent the little guy. We were a legal behemoth, that, like a menacing bodyguard, could protect you against harm or inflict pain on your enemies if so ordered.

Baylor closed like a coach at halftime. "The firm's ability to function at such a high level depends on the talent and diligence of its associates. You are the engine that keeps the firm running!"

The Germans and a few others erupted in a burst of excited applause. What most of the rest of us had in common was that we had *not* found something to be excited about. By default, we'd chosen big law firm practice primarily because it paid well, not because we were excited about drafting complex discovery motions in multi-jurisdictional litigation for the next thirty years. We were at Latham because, if we were going to be associates in a big firm, the previous summer had convinced us that Latham was the best place to do it.

The next day, we sat through hour-long presentations from each of the firm's practice departments: Corporate, Land Use, Litigation, Real Estate, and Tax. Jim Arnold, our friendly, beer-bonging recruiting partner from our summer at Latham, gave the Corporate Department presentation. As he strode through the crowd toward the stage, the LA office stubs hooted and hollered. "A-R-N-O-L-D," someone called out in a low voice. Others flashed LA office gang signs. Really. But Arnold ignored his fans and kept his head focused on the floor. The humor and engaging tone of the previous summer were gone. He seemed stressed out and tired, and he barely looked up as he rushed through a presentation called "Anatomy of a Merger," which after five minutes had most of the room struggling to stay awake. When he finished, he packed up and quickly made a beeline for the door.

The litigation presentation, "Anatomy of a Lawsuit," was at least more animated. A litigation partner from the New York office paced up and down the aisles among us, enthusiastic, eyes fixed wide and unblinking, shouting through the various stages of legal conflict. "Conflict law is *real* law practice!" he yelled into the face of a recoiling stub from the Chicago office.

There was too much ground being covered too quickly for us to absorb many details. Each presentation was an entire semester of law school in one hour. But that, I figured, wasn't the point. There were themes and buzzwords in each presentation that we were meant to internalize. As junior associates, we were supposed to work "efficiently" and "diligently," with "attention to detail" on every task, no matter how tedious or mundane it may seem to us. We were to think through even the smallest details, forward and backward. We were to proofread everything twice and triple-check every citation. "Nothing goes out the door here without being analyzed from every angle. We think ten steps ahead of our enemies."

At this point, most of us were bored stiff. People began to wander off for extended "bathroom breaks" that involved watching football or napping in their rooms. A group of us planned to skip the last two presentations, on tax and pro bono, to watch the USC football game in the lobby bar. The Tax Department was generally considered the most boring of the practice groups, made up of nerdy back-office people who couldn't bring in their own clients and who fed off the need for tax advice in corporate deals. And how much trouble could I get into for skipping out on the pro bono program? Pro bono work—unpaid legal assistance to low-income clients—was something I figured law firms only claimed to care about to enhance their public image. Besides, if I had wanted to be a public-interest lawyer, I wouldn't have come to Latham.

Our escape plan worked for about an hour, until Susan Clark, the firm's head administrator and the person in charge of LWU, walked by the lobby bar and spotted about twenty of us drinking beer and watching football. We were marched back into the conference room like misbehaving schoolchildren just as the pro bono presentation was beginning.

Mark Hensler, a partner on Latham's Pro Bono Committee, was explaining the firm's commitment to this work. Pro bono publico—for the public good—is a tradition of the legal profession founded on the idea that every lawyer should devote at least a portion of his or her time to representing indigent clients or worthy causes for free. Like every major law firm, Latham had an organized pro bono program in which young attorneys were encouraged to take on projects approved by the firm and supervised by more experienced attorneys. Firms do this for the good of the community, to provide hands-on experience for junior attorneys, and because there is overwhelming peer pressure within the legal profession to do it. From a public-relations standpoint, pro bono is a very big deal for law firms. Legal publications rate firms' pro bono programs, and firms tout their pro bono programs and the pro bono successes of their attorneys to their clients and recruits.

The majority of pro bono cases handled by Latham and other big firms involve relatively simple immigration, family, or misdemeanor issues, the kind of things one or two junior attorneys can handle in a few weeks. "It's a good way to get hands-on legal experience as a junior associate," Hensler said.

I sat there half-listening, bitter about missing the game.

On Sunday morning, we were piled into buses and taken for a day of team-building activities at a park outside of Reston. It felt good to get out of the meetings, but there was a general consensus that this team-building thing was lame and meant for middle-school kids, sorority girls, or weak-minded professionals who couldn't accomplish things on their own. Teamwork is not something in most lawyers'—particularly young lawyers'—DNA. And the Latham stubs, accustomed to being at the top of their class, were looking for ways to stand out from the pack, not join it.

The counselors divided us into teams and gave us tasks meant to require teamwork and communication to accomplish: getting every team member onto a small wooden square, building a soap-box car from odd materials. Quickly, my team degenerated into a *Lord of the Flies* sequel, as the alphas and wannabe alphas tried to assert themselves and everyone else refused to take direction or cooperate. The counselors tried to help, but were pushed aside and their advice ignored. By the end of the day we had failed miserably at every task, and our counselor was a broken man, looking as though he had just witnessed a bad auto accident.

The final activity before we returned to our offices to start our legal careers was the friendship circle, where I held hands with Igor. It felt ridiculous at the time: a group of adults standing in a circle, holding hands. We were lawyers, not eighth-graders. We didn't need to hold hands; we didn't even need to be friends. But it was fitting, in a way. We were starting our Latham career together, as equals. Despite what some of us may have thought privately, at this point, there were no superstars, no one was on the partnership track, no one had been designated a slacker. We were Latham's associate class of 2001, and for several years, like high-school freshmen, we would climb the ranks together—junior associates for two years, then mid-level associates from our third to our fifth years, and senior associates in years six and seven. In our eighth year, those who remained from our class would be eligible to be considered for partnership.

We were bonded, at this point, by what we did not know. Despite three years of law school and a summer at Latham, most of us had little idea what real day-to-day law practice was like. Our summer associate experience had been about recruiting, and Latham had gone to great expense and effort to distract us from seeing the reality. Our law school education had been an intellectual exercise, teaching us to "think like lawyers" and, to a certain extent, teaching us what the law was, but telling us almost nothing about the practice of law. For example, I knew what a complaint was, but I had no idea how to draft or file one.

But like the link between Igor and me, our bond was delicate. We had all come to Latham for our own reasons, with our own personalities and ambitions. We would be measured against one another, in how many hours we billed, the type of work we were doing, how much responsibility we took on. The defining statement in our associate reviews would be "Is [associate X] performing at a level consistent with his class?" This would breed jealousy, passive-aggressive maneuvering for the best assignments, and in some cases, outright hostility.

And statistically, we wouldn't stay bonded for long. Through a combination of voluntary and involuntary departures, 20 percent of us would leave the firm by the end of our first year, 40 percent by the end of the second. About 80 percent of us wouldn't make it to our fifth year. And by the eighth year, when we were up for partnership, only a handful of us, maybe one or two in each office, would remain.

CHAPTER 4

Baby Sharks

LOS ANGELES, OCTOBER 2001

I AM LIVING NEAR the beach in Santa Monica, in a two-bedroom apartment I share with Matt Barnes, one of my friends from the previous summer and a fellow stub. It's exciting to be back in LA, and I'm looking forward to starting work and seeing friends from the past summer.

Matt started work the week before, and I haven't seen much of him. On returning from LWU, he went straight from the airport to the office. As far as I can tell, he has not been back to the apartment, which means he is either still at the office or hung over in some girl's apartment. Matt seems resolved not to let his career interfere with his nightlife. He lives on fumes, getting up at 5:00 A.M. to work out, working late, and then storming the bars and nightclubs of Hollywood and Santa Monica like a social bulldozer running on vodka and soda, charging up to attractive girls fearlessly, introducing himself as "the half-Asian," or "zero-point-five," and offering to show them which parts are Asian and which parts not. Amazingly—or maybe not, since he is an athletic, good-looking guy with a Harvard Law degree and a six-figure job—girls find him charming. He doesn't sleep so much as collapse from exhaustion for a few hours. And he likes it that way.

All Matt has said about work so far is, "It's a different place, bro. You'll see."

I ARRIVED AT Latham's main reception, on the fortieth floor, at a few minutes after eight. Our day wasn't scheduled to begin until eight thirty, but most of the forty-seven other stubs were already there, and the lobby buzzed with nervous energy. Most of us had been summer associates together, so it was a reunion of sorts. I nodded to familiar faces as I moved through the crowd to the couch area, where my friends Trevor Wilson and Mike Wilke were sitting with a few others.

"Loogat dis fuggin guy," Wilke greeted me in his Long Island accent, smacking me on the back so hard my teeth rattled. "You ready for this, Graham?" Trevor was doubled over with laughter as Jeff Hicks was explaining that the bright red Hawaiian shirt with denim sleeves he had selected for his first day of work was his own design. "Yep, I designed this baby myself. Pretty sweet, huh?"

It was a sign of the times. A few years earlier, Latham and most other West Coast law firms had adopted a "business casual" dress code to help them compete for talent against the dot-coms, whose employees wore shorts and flip-flops. While this was popular with a lot of Latham's young recruits, taking away their dark-suit uniforms gave lawyers a broader choice, and that was not necessarily a good thing for a lot of them. A few of the older ones had even given up and gone back to wearing suits every day.

As we milled around, Brooke Levin, a third-year associate who had taken us to dinner and drinks a half-dozen times the previous summer, walked through the lobby. "Hey, Brooke!" we called out and waved. Brooke never broke stride. She turned her head and stared at us for a moment, showing no recognition, and kept walking.

"What the fuck was that?" Wilke said as we stood there frozen in mid-wave.

"Jeeesusss," Trevor whispered, "I guess the recruiting really is over. Welcome to the *real* Latham."

Maybe it was a statement that recruiting was over and that stubs like us shouldn't be hollering and waving at third-year associates, or maybe Brooke just wasn't wearing her contact lenses. But combined with Jim Arnold's performance at LWU weekend, her response stirred an uncomfortable thought: *Maybe this isn't the same place, and these aren't the same people we saw last summer.*

At exactly 8:30, someone from Human Resources rounded us up and herded us down the elevators to the sixth floor, where we shuffled past a picture of the Hindenburg exploding in flames and into Conference Room C to begin our legal careers. Waiting for us in the center of the room was Elaine Sherman, the managing partner of the LA office. In her early fifties, well-coiffed, and intense, Elaine was one of the most powerful people in the office, and therefore, to me, terrifying. In my one brief conversation with her the previous summer,

I'd felt as if I had been pulled over by the cops and they were running my plates. The rumor among the associates was that she had been appointed managing partner to restore order to the LA office after a wild spell in the 1980s and early '90s, when, so the rumor went, lawyers were doing cocaine off their desks, and empty conference rooms were serving as informal red-light districts. (The word was that former Latham associates had written for *L.A. Law* and had used real stories for some of the more sensational plot lines.) It was hard to imagine Latham ever being *that* wild, but if it had been, Elaine seemed the perfect antidote. She parted her lips and flashed her teeth in what I took to be a smile and welcomed us to the firm by getting right down to business: "Despite the rumors you might have heard about the economy and layoffs, we *are* happy to see you. And we do not have any current plans for layoffs."

Immediately a hand shot up.

"When you say 'no *current* plans,' does that mean the firm is or will be contemplating layoffs in the future?" asked Lauren Baker, the former president of the *UCLA Law Review.*

Elaine paused and smirked, as if at the skinny little stub's boldness. "I can't predict the future, but as of right now, we have no plans for layoffs."

Another hand.

"So the firm would consider laying off associates in the future? Is there a timetable for making a decision? Will we be updated?" This was from Megan Sullivan, from Chicago Law.

I was surprised by my stubmates' readiness to challenge the managing partner on their first day, and about something that she had just assured us was not under consideration. It was a down economy and we were lucky just to have jobs. But newly hired associates, I would learn, often come into big law firms eager to show off their lawyering skills, and with an inflated view of their worth and bargaining leverage. The following year, a stub from Stanford would attempt to lead a revolt via firm-wide email over Latham's decision to take away the associates' $5,000 office decorating budget. Another stub that year threw a tantrum at a meeting over the fact that the firm's firewall prevented him from going on eBay while at work. It's the nature of the beast. These were accomplished people, most having been top students at top law schools, trained to argue and eager to seek out injustice, real or perceived, and to be heard: baby sharks looking to sharpen their teeth. If Latham wasn't going to pay top-of-the-market salaries, or was going to drop ominous hints about layoffs, these people were sure they had other options. And having been fawned over the previous summer, they were sure their departure would be crushing to Latham.

Elaine brushed off the questions by explaining that despite the economic slowdown, Latham was in the middle of the busiest and most prosperous period in its history. And we, the firm's largest stub class ever, were expected to step in and help shoulder the workload. "You are here because we believe every one of you is a Latham-quality lawyer. Everyone in this room is intelligent and capable of doing excellent work. We assume that you will be careful and diligent at each task for each matter you work on. Attention to detail is *very* important here." And then, having more important things to do, she turned us over to a partner on the firm's Associates Committee—the "Ass. Com.," which monitored associates' hours and conducted our performance reviews.

"You are required to record your time in six-minute increments," he told us, handing out examples of our time sheets: white pages with 240 little boxes representing every six minutes of a twenty-four-hour day. "It's critically important that you do your time currently and that you turn in your time sheets at the end of every day."

He didn't tell us exactly what, or how much, we were supposed to record as billable time. I would learn that no lawyer ever wants to discuss that subject, because there is no one answer. What goes into those six-minute boxes, and how many of them are filled out, can be very subjective. But I didn't know that on my first day, and the Ass. Com. partner only gave us generalities.

"You bill whenever you're working or thinking about a client matter," he said. "Be honest. That is the most important thing. Never inflate or discount your time. You are expected to work efficiently, but if something takes you ten hours to finish that you think should have taken you only five, put in for ten. It's the partner's job to make any necessary adjustments to the bill, not yours. We are in the business of client service, and billable hours are our product. It's an important part of what we do."

The Ass. Com. partner explained that the sluggish economy had done little more than shift the weight of the work at Latham among the departments. The Corporate Mergers and Acquisitions group had been hit hardest and had slowed to *only* 100 percent of "pace"—i.e., the firm's budgeted minimum of 1,900 billable hours a year for associates. The Bankruptcy and Litigation departments, however, were going flat-out—which sounded ominous—with most associates in those departments billing between 110 and 160 percent of pace. I doodled on the notepad in front of me: 160 percent of 1,900 equaled 3,040 hours a year, which broke down to almost 60 hours a week, 52 weeks a year, without counting commuting time and firm meetings.

Though we were required to bill a minimum of 1,900 hours a year, most associates billed between 2,000 and 2,600 hours. Again, I did the math: 10 billable hours a day times 5 days a week times 52 weeks a year equaled 2,600. And those were only *billable* hours. Another 20 to 30 percent of our time would be unbillable—spent in firm meetings, recording our time, and sitting on the LA freeways going to and from work. So unless we seriously padded our hours, the upper figure was *not* 2,600, but possibly as many as 3,380 total hours spent on work alone: the equivalent of 9 hours a day, 7 days a week, 52 weeks a year.

For two years, we would be "unassigned associates"—not assigned to specialized departments—and thus fair game to anyone. Any assignments we received would come from "The Book," the compilation of all matters that needed more staffing by associates. "But you should be proactive as well," the Ass. Com. partner continued. "If you have additional capacity, email The Book for new assignments or knock on partners' doors and introduce yourself. It is your responsibility to stay on pace."

Twice a year the Associates Committee would meet to review our billable hours and comments from our supervising attorneys. Then a partner or senior associate from the Ass. Com. would tell us how we were doing and give us "the message" from the committee. "We take these reviews seriously, and so should you," he said. He didn't say it, but we all knew that a single less-than-great review could knock an associate off the partnership track, and a bad review from a partner could torpedo an associate's career at the firm.

Next we were whipped through training on Westlaw and Lexis, complicated legal research programs seemingly designed for maximum user confusion. If used incorrectly, they can easily run a client's bill through the roof. We were then given a binder with our firm ID cards and codes and told to go to our offices and await our first assignments.

On the way to my office, I began leafing through the binder. The first page, with my name printed at the top, held the most important information I'd received all day. I was Latham attorney number 07249. I would need this number every time I logged on to the firm's computer system, filled out a time sheet, performed Lexis or Westlaw research, or signed in for lunch at the firm's cafeteria. "Joe Theisman, Ken Griffey, Jr., Ted Williams"—7, 24, 9—I repeated, committing the number to memory.

My office was on the thirty-seventh floor, office number 3737, and my secretary's name was Debbie. In the pocket of the binder was a magnetized key card for using the elevator and getting into each of the firm's floors, which were secured by locked glass doors. I got into an elevator and headed for thirty-seven. After fumbling with my key card and pushing through the glass doors, I'd taken no more than ten steps when I heard a string of names paged over the loudspeaker, including mine. I remembered from the previous summer that people were constantly being paged throughout the day, but I had never been paged before and had no idea what to do. I picked up my pace until I spotted my office, with the silver nameplate next to the door. I dropped my binder and other orientation materials on my desk and picked up the phone. Not knowing what else to do, I pressed zero.

"Operator."

"Hi. I was just paged. This is my first day, and I'm not sure what to do."

"Hold please."

(New voice) "Paging."

"Hi. I was just paged. This is my first day, and I'm not sure what to do."

"What's your name?"

"Ian Graham"

"Are you in the office, Mr. Graham?"

"Yes."

Click.

Thirty seconds later, my office phone rang. Julianne Wang, a fourth-year associate in the Litigation Department, was calling from her cell phone as she drove. "Did you get the email from Doreen?" she asked. I told her we had just finished orientation and I hadn't even had a chance to turn on my computer. "You should probably do that," she said dryly. "There should be a forwarded email from me to you and a few other first-years explaining the assignment. If you have any questions, call me. Otherwise, I'll see you in San Diego tomorrow."

When I finally got my computer going, I found an email to me and five other stubs with the subject line "First Assignment—SD Document Review Team." The San Diego office needed some help reviewing documents for a healthcare case. We were to get ourselves to Latham's San Diego office by eight thirty the next morning and await further instructions. We could drive or take the train, business class. The firm had reserved rooms for us at the U.S. Grant Hotel downtown. Attached to the email were two documents, one a twenty-page subpoena from the U.S. Attorney's Office that we were to read and bring with us to San Diego. The second, labeled "Billing Instructions," explained that we were to bill all time and expenses to a ten-digit client matter number.

As I was printing out the subpoena, Trevor and Mike walked in. They had been recruited for this assignment as well, and they'd seen my name on the email.

"So I guess we're healthcare lawyers, whatever that means," Trevor said with a smile.

"Go home and grab your shit," Mike barked. "My secretary put us all on the seven o'clock train."

I had been in my office less than five minutes. Before leaving, I took a minute to look around. The room was about fifteen feet long by ten feet wide, with an L-shaped built-in desk that started on my left and doglegged into the middle of the room. Empty cabinets and drawers ran the length of one wall. Two chairs sat in front of my desk, and behind the desk a wall of windows faced northwest. The air was unusually clear for LA. Looking to the left, I could see the rooftop pool of the Standard Hotel a few blocks away, and beyond that, a corner of the Staples Center, where the Lakers play. To the right, if I pressed up against the glass, I could just make out the blue rooftop of Dodger Stadium.

From high above, the hills of Highland Park and East LA looked serene. I knew very little about that area, except that you didn't want to run out of gas or break down there on your way to or from a Dodgers game.

—~—

CHAPTER 5

Monkey Scribe

I believe in the Rolex Daytona (Black Face), the Porsche Carrera GT, mega yachts, supermodels (or rough facsimiles thereof)...and the yearning of my soul for something more.

—Anonymous big-firm lawyer/blogger

On the train to San Diego, Trevor, Mike, and I drank the complimentary Amtrak wine and tried to make sense of the government's subpoena. It was a request for documents relating to various doctors and diseases. There were at least fifty different Medicare diagnosis codes, and something called "cost reports" were mentioned repeatedly. There were more than thirty densely worded requests, each with several subparts, all of them using broad terms such as "relating to," "in connection with," and "in reference to."

"I hardly understand a word of this," Trevor said.

"Yeah, this looks awful," Mike agreed.

"At least we get to stay in a nice hotel!" I said.

The Amtrak wine was plentiful but poisonous. After only a couple of glasses, I woke up the next morning with no idea where I was. My head felt like a beaten piñata.

When we met in the lobby the next morning, Trevor, who also looked like hell, was mumbling something about his head. We ordered coffee to go and headed to the office, where we met three other Latham stubs from LA: Paul Martin, Tom Lee, and Eric Chang. Lee had been a summer associate in Latham's New York office the year before. Martin and Chang had summered elsewhere and were new to the firm. Lee and Martin seemed friendly. Chang had the unreadable expression of a poker player and shook hands with us without a word. Trevor whispered, "Chang was in my section at UCLA. Weird dude."

A few minutes later a paralegal fetched us, and we followed her upstairs to a windowless conference room that she called "the opium den" and then began laughing hysterically. Three San Diego associates were already there and had been the whole night, it appeared, from their disheveled clothing and thousand-yard stares. They nodded as we entered, glad to see help arrive. Cardboard boxes covered the huge conference table, and hundreds more were stacked along the walls. Twelve sheets of white paper were posted along the far wall, each with the name of a different person on it. We stood there in awkward silence until Trevor spoke up.

"I'm just a stub and all, but I'm guessing the guys on the wall are pretty much fucked."

"Something like that," said Julianne, entering the room behind us. She handed us another fifteen-page subpoena from the U.S. Inspector General's Office to our client, an HMO being investigated for fraudulently overbilling Medicare. Our job, Julianne said, was to review every piece of paper in every box and pull any documents that were responsive to any of the more than thirty requests in the first subpoena, or the twenty requests in the second, or that contained any of the names posted around the room. For each document we pulled, we were to fill out a form, listing which request the document was responsive to and signing our name at the bottom. "Billing instructions are in the email you received. Submit all receipts for dinners and travel to your secretaries for reimbursement. Any questions?"

I had a few, like "What is a cost report?" and "Can you explain Medicare?" But I kept quiet. After a beat came the only question: "Do you have any good restaurants in San Diego, like Spago in LA?" from Jeff Sanders, a late-arriving LA stub.

"Shut the fuck up, Jeff," I heard Paul Martin whisper to him amid disgusted groans and eye-rolling from the San Diego attorneys who had been working through the night and had now pegged us as typical LA types, more concerned with fancy dinners than work—which wasn't altogether inaccurate.

"I'm sure these guys can help you with that," Julianne said, nodding to the San Diego associates. She thanked us for coming and told us lunch would be brought into the conference room at noon so that we could work straight through. Then she left.

Each box held thousands of documents. There were now more than fifty broadly worded requests for documents in the subpoenas. It was our first full day of law practice, and none of us knew anything about the healthcare industry or the issues involved in the case.

"Shoot me in the face," Mike Wilke muttered as we sat down at the table.

It took me most of the first day to get through one box. In response to the subpoena, our client had sent every document that could possibly relate in any manner to any of these requests, including emails, billing records, patient medical reports, and other unidentifiable business records. My first box contained thousands of pages of Medicare billing reports and emails from hospital staff, all laced with incomprehensible codes and industry jargon. Each page in each box had to be compared carefully to the fifty requests in the subpoena and inspected to see if it contained any of the names posted on the wall or the names and/or email addresses of a list of attorneys. In some cases, it took me close to an hour to review a single page.

It was mind-numbing work, but there was a feeling of camaraderie in the conference room. Jeff Sanders's question, ill timed as it was, caught our mood. We were still excited at staying in fancy hotels and dining at expensive restaurants on the client's dime. We laughed and joked amiably about how hard we had worked to get here just to do mindless work. Except for Eric Chang.

Chang was not so amiable. He didn't say a word in the conference room for the first several days and kept to himself in the evenings. Finally, on Friday, apparently sick of our chatter, he spoke up. "You think this is funny?" he snarled. "If I'd known I was going to be a glorified secretary, I would have taken a job on Wall Street where I'd be making a lot more money. $125,000 may look like good money to us, but broken down by the hour, at 2,600 billable hours a year we're making, like,

$40 an hour. That's what I pay my cleaning lady!" He jabbed his finger into the table for emphasis. "The firm bills us out to clients at $250 an hour, and even if half that amount goes for overhead, we've paid for our salary after 1,100 hours. Every hour we bill after that is profit for the partners. We're just units of income!" When he finished, he put his head down and resumed working in silence.

"Eric Chang, ladies and gentlemen," Trevor whispered to Mike and me.

It would have taken us years to look carefully at each document. I figured this was why there had been so much emphasis on "diligence" and "attention to detail" at our orientations. The work was so tedious that it was tempting to turn off your brain and just coast. We tried to stay attentive, but by the middle of the second week, we all felt brain-dead and nobody cared anymore. By consensus, we started taking a narrower approach, tossing out every document as unresponsive to the subpoenas unless something in it jumped out at us. And the pace picked up. By the end of the second week, we were starting to think we could finish in another two or three weeks.

The following Monday, a paralegal quietly wheeled in a stack of new boxes, and then another, and another. "You didn't know?" she asked, seeing the pained expressions of surprise on our faces. "There's an entire warehouse full of these. Like, thousands more."

And so, for the next few months, the routine was the same. Every Sunday night, I would take the seven o'clock Surfliner down to San Diego, review documents all week, and return on the eleven o'clock train Friday night. It wasn't difficult work by any stretch—"easy hours," the more senior attorneys called it. But within a few weeks, we had eaten at every fancy restaurant in San Diego, the novelty of hotel life was wearing off, and cramped in a conference room together for more than twelve hours a day, we were starting to get on one another's nerves. Arguments flared up over reality television, sports, and other trivial things, to the point where Chang and a second-year associate from the San Diego office couldn't even be in the same room with each other. Chang began reviewing his boxes in a storage closet.

In addition to the document review, most of us were also being peppered with other assignments from The Book. "John Rodin needs you for a five-to-ten-hour research project to be completed by Friday," or "Joe Cathey needs emergency research for a hearing by tomorrow." Most nights, after finishing in the conference room, I would work into the early morning hours in the San Diego office's law library, and on most weekends I would go into the LA office to research and write memos for these other assignments.

It wasn't *all* bad during those first months. On the nights and weekends I had free, life was good. Life was great, actually. I had money to dine at expensive restaurants and run up hundred-dollar bar tabs without batting an eye. I bought a BMW and started dating a cute blonde who lived in the apartment across the hall. But getting a small taste of the good life in LA only made the long hours at the office more painful. Most of my nonlawyer friends weren't making the money I was, but they had time to meet up for happy hour during the week, to surf on weekends, and to go out at night.

To compensate for what I was missing, I bought things. During breaks at work I found myself shopping online, looking for expensive toys to remind myself why I had taken this job. I bought a Cartier watch, a surfboard, a set of golf clubs I never got to use, and a flat-screen television I rarely watched. I had earned them, I figured, and so far, spending power was the only real perk of my job.

I wasn't the only one with the spending bug. As the paychecks rolled in, the associates' parking garage began to resemble a German car dealership, with BMWs and Mercedes in almost every space. Some people do yoga or eat chocolate to make themselves feel better. Lawyers buy things. It's is a reminder that despite the impossible hours and tedium of the job, they can afford eighty-dollar socks and thousand-dollar car payments. And as they claw their way up the ladder, they buy more and more. Before they know it, they're in golden handcuffs, unable to imagine living without a huge income. At this point, an expensive watch and a few toys didn't have me in chains yet, but I could feel myself becoming very comfortable with my paycheck.

IN THE OFFICE ELEVATOR one Saturday, I ran into Steve Newman, a short, round-faced, intense seventh-year litigation associate for whom I had done some research the previous summer. Steve seemed like a decent guy, but I had heard recently about his reputation for being tough on junior associates and for writing bad reviews.

"You busy?" he asked.

It was a common elevator question, the only appropriate response to which was, "Yes, totally slammed." Anything else and you risked getting yourself assigned more work, or worse, looking like dead weight.

"I'm totally slammed," I said. "I'm doing a big doc review and doing research for Rodin, Cathey, and a few others on some of their cases," I told him.

"Great," he said. "I need some help on one of my cases. I'll email you tomorrow."

When I arrived at the office in San Diego on Monday morning, there were ten or so emails from Steve waiting for me. The client was an insurance company being sued for *allegedly* failing to pay benefits to an elderly man, resulting in his loss of sight. Steve wanted me to research a few legal issues and to send him summaries and analyses of the cases I found. And so, in San Diego that week, in addition to reviewing documents ten hours a day and then doing the other research assignments, I stayed at the office past 2:00 A.M. most nights working on Steve's case.

Meanwhile, I was also getting assignments from a partner, Dan Sutton. It was my first direct interaction with a partner, and I was determined to do a good job. On a Friday, Sutton asked me to pull together a list of documents from the case file over the weekend and send them to him and the client in preparation for mediation that Monday. I worked around the clock all weekend to find the documents, double-check that they were the right ones, write a cover memo, and send them off. I thought I'd done a decent job and might get to sleep normally for a few days during the mediation.

On Monday morning, I arrived to find an email from the senior associate on the case to Dan, the partner, and the entire team on the case including other associates, paralegals, and secretaries that read something like: "Dan, I apologize for Ian. I don't know why he sent those documents to the client. He was not authorized to do so and there is no excuse. I expressly told him not to. I have no idea what he was thinking. He is new and clearly doesn't get it. I will make sure it is handled appropriately. I'll get him off the case."

Frantically, I went back through the emails from the associate and Dan, trying to see what I had done wrong. Had I missed something? Dan, the partner, had asked me to send the documents to him and the client. What was I supposed to do? As far as I could tell, I had done it just as I had been asked. What was the problem? And if I had messed up, why on earth did he have to include *everyone* in his email. I began to write a response to all the addressees on the email, explaining what I had done and trying to exonerate myself, but it seemed petty to involve a partner, who was in the middle of mediation, in associate bickering.

Over lunch I explained the situation to Trevor and Matt, to get their take on what I should do. "*Don't* email everyone," Trevor said. "You're not going to win a pissing contest with him. I'd speak to him directly, give him a chance to explain, and clear it up with him first." Trevor was usually the voice of reason. "Tell him to go fuck himself," was Matt's advice.

I left a voice message asking the senior associate to call me back to discuss his email. The next day he called me back. "My bad," he said, and then hung up. He never sent a retraction email. There wasn't much I could do. When I relayed the story to my father a few days later, he laughed. "Unfortunately, blame rolls downhill in a law firm," he said. "Most lawyers aren't good managers. They've never been in a position of power until they got into a law firm and are quick to point the finger if anything goes wrong. Probably not the last time something like this will happen."

AFTER REVIEWING DOCUMENTS for six weeks in the San Diego office, I returned to the LA office looking forward to getting more substantive, interesting work. I was assigned to work on a merger of two movie studios, which sounded promising. But my task on the deal was "due diligence"—the corporate law equivalent of a document review. When one company is considering buying, merging with, or investing in another, it needs to know what is in "the target's" contracts, guarantees, financial statements, and loan agreements, in order to know what it is buying. The process of reviewing these documents is called due diligence—words that make associates cringe. It amounts to teams of associates spending long hours reading and taking notes on the fine print of densely worded documents, often for months on end.

Five other stubs and I were sent to the studio's annex, a warehouse in Encino, and told to look through all the boxes in the warehouse and take notes on "anything material" to the deal—though we were never told what the specifics of the deal were, nor what was considered to be "material." When I asked a senior associate for clarification, he handed me a diagram of the deal structure, with arrows and lines connecting more than twenty different entities, and with captions such as "convertible series A stock" and "shelf takedown of subordinated notes." We spent six hours a day aimlessly sifting through the studio's files, taking detailed notes on everything we saw.

At the same time, I was also doing due diligence on an IPO for a large real estate company in downtown LA. This required an additional six-to-twelve hours a day—on top of the time spent in Burbank—looking through more boxes of documents. The deal was worth hundreds of millions of dollars to the client, and they expected us to work mistake-free around the clock to get it done. For me and two other stubs on the deal, Wilke and Jon Davies, a tall, laid-back LA native from Harvard Law, this meant pulling all-nighters checking the fine print in thousands of real estate financing arrangements, leases, signage agreements, and insurance contracts.

The senior associate on the deal was Adam Greene, a fifth-year associate who was marching toward partnership by keeping his foot on the necks of us younger associates. Greene routinely kept us at work all night to proofread temporary edits in soporifically tedious side agreements that, if the deal actually went through, might find their way into the back pages of a 150-page document that no one—literally, not a single soul—would *ever* read in its entirety. Greene would flare up at the slightest error or if something took longer than he thought it should. At one point, Jon Davies, who had recently had spinal surgery and had to pop Vicodin every six hours for the pain, accidentally transposed two numbers after working three straight all-nighters to input Greene's edits into an offering memorandum. Greene went ballistic and stormed out of the conference room screaming, "Fucking Christ! No more goddamn transposed numbers!"

To be fair, Greene was working harder than the rest of us. He seemed in constant fear—perhaps justifiably—that any mistake by him or us would get him fired, or at least wreck his chances of making partner. He stayed at the office for four-day stretches, wearing the same clothes and occasionally napping on a beanbag in his office. He lost weight, and his skin would break out when things got really tense.

This was what I had to look forward to.

I spent the first four months of my legal career this way, numbly looking at documents I did not understand, on subjects and for deals I knew little about, with almost no thought required. I felt like Yossarian, the antihero of *Catch 22*, idly censoring all adjectives out of soldiers' letters home. I hadn't expected to be coddled, and I knew I would be working hard. I just didn't know the work was going to be so seemingly meaningless and boring. I wasn't like a medical intern who works long hours but sees patients and the tangible results of his or her work. I had almost no sense of the client, of what was at stake, of the bigger picture or the strategies of any of the cases or deals I was working on. I wasn't dealing with people but with paper, endless pages of corporate fine print. There was no legal theory and hardly any legal analysis involved in any of it. I had no idea whether anything I did had helped in any way, and if it had, whether it had contributed anything I could feel good about. As a junior associate, the only skill required seemed to be a very high tolerance for boredom.

I didn't learn much about being a lawyer during those first months, but I began to absorb the real law firm culture, not the sugarcoated summer associate version. When I left the office each night, many of the senior associates were still at their desks. The twenty-four-hour document support center was humming with activity, and associates were dropping off documents to be proofed or edited overnight. The collegial atmosphere of the previous summer was long gone. Partners and associates who had stopped by to introduce themselves, invited us to lunch, or made small talk in the hallways were different people now. They had dropped the façade of recruiting, and their faces were tired and solemn. A few of the associates I had known the previous summer were still friendly, but many of them barely acknowledged my presence. The next spring, I would learn that before the summer associates arrive, the firm holds a meeting at which all attorneys are reminded to be friendly to them, to take them to lunch or dinner, and *not* to talk about the billable hours, the drudgery, or the intensity.

By the end of my fourth month at Latham, two first-years had quit and another had left the firm under murky circumstances. The rest of us began to fall into categories. A handful of first-years were already interviewing with smaller firms or were planning to leave the profession entirely. A bigger group, about half of my first-year class, didn't love the work but planned to stick around for one or two years to make some money and maybe pay off debts before finding something more fulfilling. And a small group—the gunners, they were called—appeared unfazed by the grunt work and had tunnel vision set on partnership.

I wasn't exactly sure where I fit in at this point. After my summer at Latham, I had built such high hopes for a career and life at the firm that it was hard to imagine leaving the prestige of the job and the security of the paycheck so soon. Life and work at other law firms were not likely to be any different; my friends from law school who were at other firms were having the same experiences, and in many cases worse. And they weren't making the money I was. Maybe, I thought, the first months or years at a firm were just a boot-camp-like shock, designed to separate those who really wanted it from those who didn't. Maybe, after a while, you just get used to having no life outside of work and pulling all-nighters doing work so tedious and mindless that it makes you want to jump out a window.

But, the thing was, I didn't *want* to get used to it. I didn't want to turn into a robotic, sadistic, or stress-crazed senior associate, or even into a partner who measured his years in terms of billable hours and bonuses or his life by the size of his swimming pool and his status at the firm. *There has* got *to be another way,* I thought.

In desperation to escape from the document reviews and due diligence, and to get some substantive legal experience, I decided to volunteer for one of the firm's pro bono cases. Late one evening, I emailed the head of Latham's Pro Bono Department and asked if there were any cases that needed staffing. The next morning, one of the firm's couriers wheeled two large, battered cardboard boxes into my office. On top of one of them was a note: "Ian, please read these and call me. Bob Long."

On the side of one of the boxes, in faded black Magic Marker, was written, THE PEOPLE V. MARIO ROCHA.

—~—

CHAPTER 6

Murder in the Barrio

I HAD A LONG DAY of proofreading and shuffling papers for Adam Greene's IPO ahead of me and little interest in the newly delivered boxes. I'd never heard of Bob Long, which wasn't altogether surprising. Having spent most of my first six weeks in San Diego, I didn't even know the attorneys on the other side of my floor, much less all 300 of them spread out over the other eleven floors. I pulled up Long's profile on the firm's website, expecting to see a mid-level or perhaps senior associate along with the standard associate Web profile: one or two sentences listing his department and law school. When Long's profile came up, I stared at the screen for a moment, rubbed my eyes, and then nearly fell out of my chair.

"Robert A. Long is a senior litigation partner and a member of the firm since 1971. Mr. Long is the former Managing Partner of the Los Angeles office, with a practice focused on complex business litigation and trial practice, with a range of experience that includes state and federal court trials and arbitrations..."

The profile listed a dozen or so cases on which Long had been lead counsel for big name companies in high-stakes litigation. He had been elected a fellow of the American College of Trial Lawyers and had served on the Board of Governors of the Association of Business Trial Lawyers and the boards of prestigious companies and charitable organizations. Accompanying the profile was a head shot of an elegant man wearing a finely tailored dark suit with a perfectly knotted bow tie, with a dignified and serious expression on his face. He had a full head of salt-and-pepper hair and looked like the Hollywood image of a big-firm senior partner.

What the hell is this guy doing on a pro bono case? I wondered.

I called a third-year associate I was friendly with to get the scoop on Long. "Wow!" he said when I told him about the boxes and the note. "Congrats! Bob's a big-time powerful partner, but also a good guy. I haven't worked with him, but I've heard he's good to work for and actually kind of cool. Must be a big case. Good luck."

Big case? I thought this was pro bono.

Now I was curious. I decided Greene could wait an hour while I skimmed through the boxes to get an idea of what Long's case was about. I lifted the first box onto my desk and opened the lid. Inside were eight volumes of transcripts from a 1997 criminal trial. I picked out the first volume and started reading.

Six hours later, I had hardly moved.

HIGHLAND PARK, EAST LOS ANGELES, 1996

On a Friday afternoon in February 1996, sixteen-year-old Mario Rocha left the East LA Skills Center shortly after 3:30. He headed to the bus stop, where he caught the number 81 bus toward his mother's house on San Pasqual Avenue in the East LA neighborhood of Highland Park. The afternoon was warm and sunny, and ordinarily Mario would have lingered outside, talking to friends and making plans for the weekend. But he already had plans for the coming evening, and he wanted to get home to see his mother before she left for the weekend to visit her sister in San Diego.

Mario had grown up in Highland Park, in a neighborhood considered the territory of the Highland Park gang. His father, an airplane mechanic at Northrop Corp., lost his job when the factory shut down in the early 1980s and, after getting hit by a car and injuring his back, struggled with drug and alcohol addiction. He separated from Mario's mother when Mario was thirteen, leaving Mario's mother, Virginia, who spoke little English and worked as a school custodian, to raise her three boys by herself. Mario's brother, Danny, four years older than Mario, had joined the Highland Park gang at sixteen and had been an active member until recently, when his girlfriend became pregnant and he chose to focus on work.

At sixteen, Mario wasn't an angel, either. Although he had been placed in accelerated classes, he had dropped out of high school after his sixteenth birthday, preferring to smoke weed and hang around with his friends on the block. At fifteen, Mario was put on probation for being a passenger in a car that had been stolen by one of his friends. That was enough, along with his family history, to put him on the Northeast LAPD precinct's list of suspected Highland Park gang members.

But Mario was not a follower, and he had resisted gang life. He was repelled by the violence and gang mentality that he had seen firsthand. "Once you join a gang, you lose control of your life and your decisions," he told me later. "You always have a beef with somebody, and somebody always has a beef with you. I didn't want to spend my life looking over my shoulder."

Until recently, the Highland Park gang had been just one of the more than a hundred Latino street gangs packed into a ten-mile radius of East LA. Although considered "one of the most organized, most profitable, and most dangerous gangs in Los Angeles" by the Los Angeles city attorney's office, they were much smaller than LA's largest and most ruthless Latino gang, The Avenues.

Named for the avenues that slice across Figueroa Street, Northeast LA's bustling main drag, by the mid-1990s The Avenues had more than eight hundred members spread among cliques that claimed almost of all of Northeast LA, including Highland Park, as their territory. Police blamed The Avenues alone for over half of the more than two hundred murders in these areas in the early nineties. Beyond their numbers and violent reputation, The Avenues bolstered their power in the neighborhoods by their affiliation with Eme, the Mexican mafia. Although Eme had only a few hundred members in the mid-1990s, most of whom were incarcerated in California, they controlled most of Southern California's eighty thousand Latino gang members by controlling the prisons, offering protection for incarcerated gang members who had cooperated with them on the streets, and certain death to inmates who crossed them. The Avenues were Eme's tax men, collecting money from local gangs and drug dealers and passing it on to Eme.

In the mid-1990s, The Avenues overstepped, attracting the attention of federal law enforcement after a series of unprovoked killings of African Americans in an effort to drive blacks from their East LA neighborhoods. Their most notorious murder happened on September 17, 1995, when three-year-old Stephanie Kuhen and five of her family members were returning from a birthday party in the Northeast Los Angeles neighborhood of Cypress Park. Unfamiliar with the area and distracted by a car full of young kids, Stephanie's stepfather made a wrong turn off of Figueroa Street and onto Isabel Avenue—into an area the police called "Assassins Alley." As her stepfather tried to turn the car around, a group of The Avenues surrounded the car and opened fire, killing Stephanie instantly and seriously wounding her stepfather and younger brother.

In the days following the Kuhen murder, The Avenues made national headlines, as President Clinton publicly denounced the gang and pledged federal money to help Los Angeles curb its epidemic of gang violence. The FBI and LAPD declared a "war on gangs" and cooperated to create specialized, aggressive anti-gang police units to patrol East LA neighborhoods. Within weeks, dozens of The Avenues' leaders were arrested and charged with racketeering, hate crimes, and scores of murders, including the shooting of a fifteen-year-old boy on a bicycle; the murders of three advisors to Edward James Olmos's 1992 film, *American Me*, about the Mexican mafia; and the Kuhen killing.

Although the arrests decapitated The Avenues' leadership, the result on the street was an *increase* in violence. Twelve members of The Avenues were killed in the first two months following the crackdown, as younger gang members fought to fill vacant leadership positions. Smaller local gangs, emboldened by the decimation of The Avenues, began to fight for control of their neighborhoods. One of those rivals was the Highland Park gang.

MARIO AND HIS MOTHER had clashed over many things, especially his decision to drop out of school, but they also shared a strong bond. Virginia Rocha was thankful Mario had not followed his brother into the gang, and she secretly enjoyed having him home to keep her company. She taught him to draw and paint, which he did well. He enjoyed hearing her stories about coming to California in the late 1960s, "barefoot and bell-bottomed," as Mario would later write, from her home in Juarez, Mexico.

Virginia had tried to get Mario to go with her to San Diego that February weekend. But Mario declined, telling his mother he had been invited to a party that night by some friends from Cathedral High School, an all-boys Catholic school near downtown LA, and teasing her that he was going to meet a nice girl from Sacred Heart, Cathedral's sister school. Reluctantly, Virginia consented to let Mario stay home with his brothers.

It was almost four thirty by the time Mario's bus got to the bottom of San Pasqual. Virginia had waited for Mario as long as she could, but the rush-hour traffic that gridlocks miles of the 405 freeway to San Diego can easily turn a two-hour drive into a five-hour nightmare. Virginia left at four, still worried.

Shortly after nine thirty that night, Gabriel Ramirez and his brother Anthony pulled up in front of Mario's house in their 1991 Ford Explorer and honked the horn. The Ramirez brothers and Mario had been friends since they played Pee Wee football together as ten-year-olds. Like Mario, Gabriel and Anthony had grown up in Highland Park and had friends who were gang members, but had chosen not to join a gang themselves. Mario had been invited to the party earlier that day by his friend Damien Sanchez, a student at Cathedral High, and in turn, had invited the Ramirez brothers. Dressed casually in dark baggy jeans and a black T-shirt under a dark blue windbreaker, Mario bolted out the door and climbed into the backseat, and the three friends headed to the party on Ebby Avenue.

They could hear the music in the backyard as they walked up the driveway beside the house. A blue tarp was strung across the rear of the driveway, forming a gate to the party in back. Matthew Padilla, from Cathedral High, and Damien Sanchez stood on the street side of the tarp charging a two-dollar entry fee to help cover the cost of the keg and liquor. Mario paid for himself and his friends with the money Virginia had left him, and they entered the party.

About fifty people were already in the backyard. A deejay was set up inside the kitchen. Speakers just outside the kitchen windows blared loud hip-hop music. On one side of the yard, a large beer keg was set up next to a big cooler of vodka punch called "jungle juice." The faint scent of marijuana drifted over the yard as Cathedral boys and Sacred Heart girls bobbed their heads and danced. Mario, Gabriel, and Anthony filled plastic cups at the keg and made their way to an open space at the rear of the yard to survey the party.

On the dance floor, Martin Aceves, a leader among the Cathedral boys, had a special reason to celebrate. An honor student at Cathedral, Aceves had recently been accepted to Cal State Northridge. With his friends Lauro Mendoza and Arturo Torres and their girlfriends, Aceves danced shirtless, having the time of his life.

For more than an hour, Mario stood talking to the Ramirez brothers and a few others at the rear of the yard. Around eleven, spotting an attractive girl standing near the keg, he decided to make his move. Despite a slight pudginess to his 190-pound frame, Mario was handsome. And he was confident. Seeing that the girl's cup was almost empty, Mario offered to refill it, grabbing the nozzle of the keg. She accepted, and they struck up a conversation.

Minutes later, Mario noticed a group enter the party, one of them wearing a baseball cap with the letters *HLP* on the front. Mario knew the meaning of that hat immediately—his brother had worn one like it when he was in the Highland Park gang. Looking closely, Mario recognized two of them as gang members his brother Danny had hung out with occasionally. Mario knew them by their gang monikers: "Pee Wee" and "Cartoon."

Mario didn't think too much of it. Gang members at parties in Highland Park weren't so unusual. They were out of place in this closely knit high-school group, but Mario figured *they know who I am so they're not going to bother me.* The gatekeepers, Padilla and Sanchez, had probably been too intimidated to keep them out.

Unaware of the gang members' presence, a Cathedral High student bobbed on the dance floor wearing a California Angels baseball cap with the letters *CA* linked together on the front. The Cathedral kid didn't look or act like a gangster, but in the gang parlance of Highland Park, the letters *CA* stood for the Cypress Avenue gang, a faction of The Avenues that was a rival to the Highland Park gang.

Moments later, Arturo Torres felt a hard object jab into his ribs. Before he could look down, he heard a voice over his shoulder. "Where you from?" asked the person pressing into his side what Torres now realized was a gun. Though he wasn't in a gang, Torres knew the code. He was being "hit up," challenged to identify his gang affiliation. Startled, Torres turned to see the three gang members surrounding him.

"I'm not from anywhere," Torres said truthfully, hoping to defuse things.

"Then why don't you take off your fucking hat?" demanded the gang member holding the gun.

"It's cool," Torres stammered, taking off his Angels cap. "We're all Mexicans." Momentarily appeased, the gangster withdrew the gun, and he and the other two gang members walked away.

A few minutes later, Bryan Villalobos, another Cathedral student, was confronted by the same gang members. "I'm Pee Wee from Highland Park," one of them said, flashing a gun. "Where you from?"

Villalobos, too, realized he was being hit up and tried to defuse the situation. "I'm not from nowhere," he responded honestly. But by this time, Martin Aceves, Lauro Mendoza, and a few other Cathedral boys had noticed what was happening to their friends and were coming over to help. The gang members and the Cathedral boys squared off for a moment, until someone on the Cathedral side shouted, "TAC!" the initials of a local "tagging crew" called Tag All Cities, who spray-painted their "tag" and other graffiti around neighborhoods to mark their territory. Tagging crews are usually nonviolent, but some are affiliated with violent gangs.

Instantly Pee Wee's fist slammed into Lauro Mendoza's jaw, knocking him to the ground. As the Cathedral boys jumped in to help their friend, a violent brawl erupted, stopping the party cold. The fight quickly spread from the dance floor and across the yard toward the tarp blocking the driveway, as other partygoers stood back, pleading for the fighting to stop. Laurie Nevarez, whose aunt's house was being used for the party, and her friends screamed for help as they moved back toward the rear of the yard, where Mario and the Ramirez brothers stood watching the fight.

Less than a minute later, shortly before midnight, a volley of three or four shots cracked from the middle of the fight. Frightened screams erupted and panicked feet pounded on the pavement as terrified teenagers fled from the backyard down the driveway and toward the street, knocking the tarp aside. Seconds later, a second volley of shots rang out as someone fired down the driveway at the fleeing crowd.

Near the rear of the yard, Martin Aceves, the honor student bound for college, lay on his back with a thirty-five-caliber bullet in his chest, taking his last breaths. Anthony Moscato, another Cathedral student, ran down Ebby Avenue with blood pouring from his left hand, which had been grazed by a bullet as he fled.

The shooting made the Sunday papers, with the *Los Angeles Times* running a front-page headline: "Highland Park Gang Members Crash Party, Cathedral Honor Student Killed." With the national spotlight already illuminating LA's gang problem, there was pressure on the police to make arrests and break up the Highland Park gang as they had The Avenues. In the days following the murder, detectives from the LAPD's Northeast Division interviewed witnesses and took statements from people who had attended the party. Within a week, Raymond Rivera (Cartoon) and Richard Guzman (Pee Wee) were arrested and charged with Aceves's murder and the attempted murder of Moscato.

But the police didn't stop there. They re-interviewed witnesses, showing them pictures of every known and suspected Highland Park gang member, pressuring them to make additional identifications. They threatened to arrest witnesses who had nothing to do with the shootings if they didn't cooperate in implicating those the police believed had also participated in the crime.

Two weeks later, in the middle of the night, three policemen rammed open the front door of Virginia Rocha's house on San Pasqual Avenue. Bounding up the stairs, they burst into Mario's bedroom. Mario, unsure of what was happening, had thrown himself on the floor where he lay flat on his stomach as the policemen entered. One of the policemen kicked Mario in the head as another placed him in handcuffs. As they led Mario out of the house, the policemen passed Virginia standing terrified by her shattered front door.

One of the officers shouted over his shoulder, "We're arresting your son for murder."

—ɱ—

CHAPTER 7

Dreams of Freedom

MARIO ROCHA did not go home. Assuming it was all a mistake that would be cleared up quickly, he waived his right to an attorney. He was interrogated, charged with the murder of Martin Aceves and the attempted murder of Anthony Moscato, and locked up in LA's Central Juvenile Hall for two years while awaiting trial.

It was there that Mario's intelligence, his gift for writing, and his demeanor of innocence caught the attention of an extraordinary Catholic nun.

LOS ANGELES, LATE FALL 1999 AND BEFORE

SISTER JANET HARRIS was sixty-eight years old when she pushed through the revolving glass doors and entered the marble lobby of Latham & Watkins's downtown LA office building in the fall of 1999. She was 5'3", small-boned, with closely cropped white hair, a round winsome face, sparkling blue eyes, and a natural grace that made her look a decade or two younger. She was attractive and, for a nun, stylish. The heels of her black boots clicked as she walked across Latham's polished floor pulling behind her a small aluminum dolly holding two battered cardboard boxes, one on top of the other, held in place by a worn bungee cord. The buses had been quicker than she'd expected, and she was a half hour early for her three o'clock appointment with Bob Long.

Janet checked in with the receptionist on the fortieth floor and took a seat on a couch, watching as young people with intelligent, intense faces and armloads of documents passed through the lobby. She picked up one of Latham's promotional brochures and smiled as she read about the firm's dedication to pro bono work. She had a good feeling about this place. Things were going to work out this time. They had to. She had been trying for three years to get a competent lawyer to take the case in her boxes, and she was getting desperate. By this point, the case was as much about her life—her faith in God and humanity—as it was about Mario.

AS A CHILD GROWING UP in a working-class neighborhood of upper Manhattan, Janet Harris had dreamed of becoming an actress. She spent her weekends and summer days hanging around the Broadway theaters, staring at the poster boards for *Oklahoma!* and *South Pacific*. But one afternoon, when she tagged along with her mother to the nearby Cloisters museum of medieval art, she was captivated by the illuminated manuscripts; her awakening to the Church began. When her family moved to San Francisco, Janet entered the teaching order of the Presentation Sisters. She was seventeen and newly graduated from high school. Art, Janet liked to say, had led her to God.

After moving to Los Angeles in her forties to pursue a master's degree in communications at Loyola University, Janet took a job teaching English at a high school in a low-income, mostly Latino neighborhood near downtown LA. She was a natural teacher, taking an interest in each of her students, listening to them without judgment and talking to them with respect. Janet marveled at their natural intelligence and creativity. Most of them were tough kids from single-parent families. She felt strongly that they were as intelligent and able, if not more so, than private-school kids in the suburbs. She often quoted to them a line from one of her favorite books, *To Kill a Mockingbird*: "Fine folks are people who do the best they can with the sense they have."

Janet noticed that neighborhood kids, many of them members of the local Eighteenth Street gang, were climbing the school fence on weekends to use the school's soccer field. Instead of notifying security, she decided to watch them herself. Week after week, she observed them from the bleachers. "It was like watching a ballet," she would later recall. "I could tell who the gang members were by how they carried themselves."

The kids were initially skeptical of the white lady in the bleachers, but Janet had an almost telepathic way of connecting to teenagers, and they soon became comfortable with her presence and began opening up to her. "I could tell if they were lying to me by their body language and tone of voice, and they knew it," she said. At one point, when a rival gang member in a passing car fired shots toward the field, one of the kids pushed Janet to the ground and shielded her with his body until the shooting stopped.

The police put pressure on Janet to tell them what she knew about the gang, but she refused, saying it was not her place to talk. This earned her still more trust from the teenagers. For her master's thesis, she filmed a documentary on the Eighteenth Street and Temple Street gangs. "It was fascinating to me. I realized how naïve I was. I understood teenagers, but I didn't understand what was happening on the streets around me," she said.

Sister Janet learned about the realities and nuances of the neighborhood. Some of the kids were hardcore gang members and sociopaths. But many of them, although they wore baggy pants and talked with street slang, weren't part of a gang or criminally involved. They were merely neighborhood kids who had been labeled as gang members by the police because of the way they looked, the neighborhood they grew up in, and the friends they had known since childhood.

The more she observed and learned about these kids, the more wary Janet became of the way the police and prosecutors seemed to blindly lump them all together, branding them as "gang members" and using the words as code for "criminal." "I saw a lot of these kids being arrested for minor, petty things," Janet said. "The police and DA's office would always add a gang charge to increase the punishment. One of my students, a fourteen-year-old freshman, was arrested for smoking a cigarette! He was just sitting on the curb with his brother, minding his own business. Next thing you know, the prosecutor is calling him a gang member and charging him with loitering and criminal mischief! You think that happens in Bel Air? These kids didn't have anyone to stick up for them, so I decided to do something about it."

Word of her work with gangs and local teenagers quickly spread. Janet was offered a job with the County Probation Department, as a community liaison—a communication link between the department and the neighborhood. She also began working at Central Juvenile Hall, as the Catholic chaplain.

Deeply appalled at how many boys and girls in their mid-teens were being tried as adults and given harsh sentences, often on the basis of tenuous gang connections, Janet began speaking out against what she saw as an increasingly punitive juvenile justice system. She appeared on radio shows and at rallies, speaking about the danger of incarcerating teens in adult prisons: "Research in brain science says that the brain isn't fully developed at fourteen or fifteen. Anyone who has raised a teenager knows that they're impulsive, they're often peer-pressured, and they act sometimes before they think. Often young people don't have the moral strength to survive in the adult prison environment. Drugs are so available inside those prisons, and gang membership is often the only way to survive."

When Governor Pete Wilson, in a speech staged outside Juvenile Hall, said, "The best form of prevention is to get the message across that adult crimes carry adult price tags," Janet confronted him. "I don't agree with what you just said. Kids just don't think like that." The governor responded, "Well, I wouldn't expect a nun to understand," and walked off.

Janet became a frequent, sometimes unwelcome, visitor to Sacramento, meeting with state politicians about reforming California's juvenile justice system, which had swelled to the largest in the nation. She networked to find jobs for kids who were released from Juvenile Hall and helped kids learn skills they would need in an office setting. She was, as Edward Humes said of her in his book, *No Matter How Loud I Shout*, about a year in the juvenile court system "someone who cares more about their futures than their pasts."

Sometimes Janet's frustration with the juvenile justice system turned personal, as when one of her former students, a sixteeen-year-old girl named Silvia Sanchez, was arrested and charged as an adult for a murder she had nothing to do with, even by the prosecutor's admission. Silvia and her boyfriend had driven to the beach in the LA suburb of Venice to meet some friends. The boyfriend, several years older than Silvia and violently abusive, told Silvia he had borrowed the car from a friend. While Silvia was at the beach with friends, the car's owner confronted the boyfriend in a parking lot and demanded his car back. In a struggle for the keys, Silvia's boyfriend stabbed the owner seventeen times, killing him. Only on the way home did he tell Silvia what had happened, adding that if she said anything to anyone he would kill her and her "retard mother." Terrified, Silvia refused to talk to the district attorney, and she was charged as an accessory to the murder.

Janet went to bat for Silvia. Given that the DA's office had many other witnesses to the murder and didn't need Silvia's testimony for a conviction, Janet felt that the DA was using Silvia as example of what happens to people who don't cooperate. She met with the district attorney, pleading with him to drop the case, but he brushed her aside—saying the city was at war with gangs—and walked out. She called the state attorney general and all the other high-level politicians she knew. They all said, one way or another, "If she's innocent, the jury will let her walk."

Days before Silvia's trial was to begin, Janet confronted the prosecutor on the case, a young deputy district attorney, in the hallway of the courthouse. "How can you do this?" Janet asked her. "This isn't justice."

The prosecutor pulled Janet aside and confided, "Between you and me, I hate this case. I don't have the heart for this. This girl doesn't deserve this."

"So why are you doing it?" Janet asked.

"Because I was told to," said the prosecutor.

But once in court, that same prosecutor described Silvia to the jury "as if she were Charlie Manson," Janet said. Janet was there when Silvia was convicted and sentenced to life in prison.

The case shook Janet deeply. "What kind of faith can you have in a system that could incarcerate Silvia Sanchez for life?" she said. She was determined to help Silvia and perhaps naïve enough to think she could.

Janet spent all her political capital and wore out her welcome pleading with the DA's office to reopen Silvia Sanchez's case, badgering politicians to consider a pardon, and looking for an attorney to appeal Silvia's case pro bono. Finally, a young lawyer agreed to take a look at the case. He spent months poring over the trial transcripts and police files before calling Janet into his office to give her his assessment. The case, he agreed, was a horrible miscarriage of justice and should never have gone to trial. But it did, and the prosecutor had done a very good job. Under the law, Silvia was, technically, an accomplice, and there was very little that could be done at this stage. He added what Janet knew: once a person is convicted they no longer have the presumption of innocence and it takes a miracle to overturn the conviction, even one as obviously unjust as Silvia's.

"Loyalty to a lie," Janet called it.

For many years, Janet's main job was to oversee religious services and coordinate volunteer activities at Central Juvenile Hall. The activity closest to her heart was a writing program called InsideOUT Writers, which she and author Karen Hunt had created in 1994. The program wasn't about writing excellence, punctuation, or grammar. Instead, it focused on giving incarcerated teenagers a chance to express themselves and to feel that someone was listening. The teachers, Karen Hunt and Duane Noriyuki, a writer for the *Los Angeles Times*, didn't tell their students what to write or judge them on their content or message. Instead they listened, encouraging the students to think for themselves and to write honestly.

In mid-1996, Janet heard about a new inmate at Juvenile Hall who was gaining a reputation for writing plays in the hall's theater program. She invited him to join Duane's writing class. Janet, who often attended the classes to listen, observe, and encourage, had read about his case in the newspaper: A Cathedral High School student had been shot and killed by gang members who crashed a party in Highland Park. The student was sixteen and didn't look or carry himself like a gang member. He had no tattoos and was polite and deferential to Duane and the other staff. "I just had a sense about him: he didn't belong in this place," Janet would say.

The class had adopted a rule that new students read first. After the kids were given thirty minutes to write, Janet listened closely as Mario Rocha stood up and read:

> Night after night, I sit in my lonely room looking out my tainted window, absorbing the dark abandoned fields, and I think, what kind of life is this? I stare at the large trees that distantly shroud these buildings and think, this is not the way I want to live. In the midst of my troublesome feelings I lower my head in sadness.

Janet and the teachers never judged the kids in the writing program on the content or quality of their work, caring only that they behaved themselves and gave a decent effort. Janet knew most of them wrote about gangs and crime, the life they had lived on the streets, and the bad decisions they had made. For most, this was a tacit admission of guilt. In class after class, Mario's writing was different. He wrote about his family and his future. "He wrote truthfully. He never embroidered his thoughts," she said.

Of his time in the writing program, Mario wrote, "I searched for words to expose the cave of my soul. I poured forth my fears, doubts, and perplexities on paper, and I began to understand my life, who I was and why."

Janet was curious. Her well-trained eye told her that this kid was not a gang member. And he did not seem at all like a murderer. "Duane showed me Mario's work," she said later, "and I began to question some of the issues raised in his essays. I can get the truth out of a rock. I talked to people who had been at the party and they told me, 'Absolutely not. Mario had nothing to do with it.'"

When Janet told Mario what she had heard about his case, he was initially hesitant.

"I can tell you the same thing I told the cops," he told her.

"I didn't see who was shooting because I was hiding behind a car. I didn't have a gun on me. I didn't shoot anyone."

"I understand," Janet replied in a calm, even voice. "Believe me, I understand about that. But let's just talk about you. Do you know why you were arrested?"

"The police say they have a witness against me," Mario responded, looking her in the eye. "Someone who saw me shoot. But I didn't do it, so I guess that person is lying, or else he thinks he saw me."

With Mario's permission, Janet contacted Mario's attorney, Anthony Garcia, to offer her help in locating or talking to witnesses. Garcia seemed annoyed and told her curtly that the case against Mario was weak and that he would be acquitted.

Janet was relieved. She allowed herself to be cautiously optimistic that a jury would not convict Mario based on the testimony of one eyewitness. "I thought, *he's going to win this trial.*"

For the next year and a half, while Mario sat in Juvenile Hall awaiting trial, he continued to attend the writing classes and to develop his voice as a writer. He read relentlessly and became known around the Hall as "the guy with the books." With Duane's and Janet's encouragement, he took and passed his GED exam. He began writing to authors he admired, asking them for guidance and to send him books. Janet called Mario a "scholar of stone and steel." She believed he could have been an outstanding student and teacher under different circumstances. She got to know Mario's mother, Virginia, and his aunts, Bertha and Martha, who visited him often at Juvenile Hall.

After more than a year at Juvenile Hall, Mario wrote a poem called "Dreams":

I may not be free to do many things but nothing can stop
me from having these dreams:
Dreams of going to college and obtaining an education that
will help me achieve my aspirations;
Dreams of becoming the famous Chicano writer Mario
Rocha, and one day writing a play that will change
someone's life;
Dreams of writing a movie that will help society understand
"the barrio" and let them see the realities of "street life";
Dreams of counseling and being there for a troubled child;
Dreams of delivering the Good News of our lord to those
in need;
Dreams of spending a whole day with my family and
treasuring every single moment;
Dreams of being out there to be an uncle to my nephews,
Carlitos and Lil' Danny;
Dreams of enjoying the life of an average eighteen-year-old;
Dreams of listening to some Zeppelin in my Kenwood stereo
system, making the whole house vibrate with intensity;
Dreams of holding a girl in my arms, sharing a warm and
loving feeling;

Dreams of waking up at home and not in here;

Dreams of using this talent which I have found to connect people of all races and classes;

Dreams of living these dreams;

Dreams of freedom.

—⁓—

CHAPTER 8

God Boxed Me In

Thou shalt not be a victim. Thou shalt not be a perpetrator. Above all, thou shalt not be a bystander.

—U.S. Holocaust Memorial Museum,
Washington, D.C.

LOS ANGELES, DECEMBER 1997

SISTER JANET ATTENDED every day of Mario's two-week trial. She sat with his mother and other family members in the first row, immediately behind Mario and his two co-defendants.

The trial was held in Judge Morris Jones's courtroom in the Criminal Courts Building, a block from City Hall in downtown LA. The building is the centerpiece of the largest court system in the country. Its government-functional lobby bustles every day with a cross-section of Los Angeles: jurors, cops, parolees, lawyers, reporters, street people, and the idly curious. O. J. Simpson's 134-day trial was held there, in 1995, in Judge

Lance Ito's ninth-floor courtroom. Judge Jones's courtroom, like all the others, was worn, functional, and surprisingly small.

The DA's office had signaled the priority it was giving this case by assigning as lead prosecutor Deputy District Attorney Bobby Grace, an up-and-comer who had made his reputation in the Hard Core Gang and Family Violence divisions of the Los Angeles District Attorney's Office. Grace had won convictions in dozens of murder cases and handled many high-profile cases, including the 1996 murder charges against celebrity rapper Snoop Dogg.

It worried Sister Janet that Mario was being tried together with two known gang members. She had sat through a lot of trials, and she knew the danger of guilt by association. And from his opening statement, Bobby Grace made it clear that the prosecution intended to lump all three defendants together as gang members and make gang terror the primary theme:

> The evidence will show that *these* defendants began hitting up people at the party. And you will learn through the evidence that that is slang for—gang slang—for asking people where are you from, and that asking people that question is a prelude to trouble, to fights, and escalating even beyond that... You will hear evidence that *these* defendants ordered people at the party to take off baseball caps that offended them, that disrespected their gang, the Highland Park gang.

Despite this opening promise, the prosecutor Grace presented no evidence at all during the trial that Mario had "disrespected," "hit up," or accosted anyone. There was no evidence that he had ordered anyone to take off a baseball cap or that he was involved in the ensuing fight.

Arturo Torres—who had been accosted for wearing a California Angels baseball cap—identified Raymond Rivera (Cartoon) as the person who had pressed a gun into his ribs and "hit him up." He said nothing about Mario.

Bryan Villalobos also testified that Richard Guzman (Pee Wee) and "two of his friends," including Rivera, approached him during the party and asked him "where you from?" Villalobos said he responded that he "wasn't from nowhere," and that Guzman replied that he was "Pee Wee from Highland Park." Villalobos testified that Mario was not part of the group that hit him up.

Other witnesses testified that Rivera and Guzman had started the fight with Lauro Mendoza. Not a single witness testified that Mario was involved in the fight.

Another witness, Nigel Lobban, testified that he was watching the fight and saw Guzman pull a gun from his waistband and fire a shot at Martin Aceves (the murder victim) from a distance of a few feet.

Regarding the second shooter, who fired down the driveway and hit Anthony Moscato in the hand, José Plascencia, a Cathedral student, testified that he had witnessed Rivera in the driveway firing a gun toward the crowd as they scattered. Peter Barragon, another partygoer, described Rivera as the person he saw shooting in the driveway. Barrragon also testified that he had known Mario since they were kids and was sure Mario was not the driveway shooter.

Apparently, these witnesses convinced the prosecutor. Later, at the end of the trial, Bobby Grace would argue in his closing statement to the jury:

> Clearly, Defendant Rivera is shooting in the driveway. What facts support that? He is shooting at individuals in the driveway based on his description. Consistently, among all the witnesses that testify, his description consistently comes up as the individual that was shooting in the driveway...Defendant Rivera is the only one the witnesses talk about...he is the individual who is seen shooting down the driveway.

Not a single witness testified to seeing more than two shooters. A police ballistics expert testified that a thirty-five-caliber bullet was recovered from Martin Aceves's body, and a twenty-two-caliber bullet was recovered from a wall inside the house. According to the LAPD's expert, this indicated that "two guns were fired."

Prosecutor Grace asked if there could have been a third gun that didn't expend a shell, such as a revolver, and the expert testified that there "could have been."

That's their case? Janet thought. *There could have been?*

A police gang expert testified that Guzman and Rivera were known, documented Highland Park gang members and that their gang monikers were Pee Wee (Guzman) and Cartoon (Rivera). He said nothing about Mario. Not a single witness testified that Mario was a gang member or was involved in the hitting-up incident or the fight that preceded the shootings.

So far, the prosecution's own witnesses appeared to be exonerating Mario.

The only evidence implicating Mario came from three witnesses. Bryan Villalobos, a Cathedral High School student, testified that he had picked Mario out of a sixteen-pack photo lineup card—a sea of similar Latino faces—as someone who "looks like" the person he saw shooting down the driveway into the crowd as people fled. However, he added that he was "not sure" of his identification and "never saw [Mario] with a weapon at any time." Legally, that was a non-identification. Villalobos also testified that he was a habitual marijuana smoker who had smoked marijuana every day for the past six years, that he had smoked marijuana the night of the party, and that he had drunk several cups of beer before the shooting. And he was unable to identify Mario in court.

Lauro Mendoza testified that after hearing the first gunshots, he was running down the driveway toward the street when he caught a "glimpse" of the person shooting toward Moscato. Mendoza saw the side of the shooter's face for "a few seconds" and could not describe what the shooter was wearing, nor his height or weight. Mendoza admitted that immediately after the shooting, he told the police that he did not see anything. However, four days later, he identified Mario from the sixteen-pack photo lineup card as the person "that looks like the guy I saw shooting the gun." Again, legally, this was a non-identification.

The only witness to implicate Mario with any degree of certainty was Matthew Padilla. Padilla testified that he was standing in the driveway on the street side of the tarp, collecting an entrance fee and acting as a gatekeeper to the backyard, when he heard voices in the backyard getting louder and "it seemed like something was happening." At that moment, he heard gunshots and "people began running through the tarp toward the street."

Padilla testified that he stayed on the street side of the tarp and stepped aside to avoid being run over by the people fleeing toward the street. From that vantage point, Padilla said he "peeped out" and saw a person "come to the middle of the driveway, get down on his right knee, place a gun in his left hand, and start firing down the driveway." Padilla acknowledged that the driveway was "dark," that he was not wearing his glasses at the time, and that in his police station interview shortly after the shooting, he had identified someone other than Mario in a six-pack photo lineup card. Yet Padilla identified Mario in court as the person he saw shooting in the driveway. He said he was "certain."

Janet was familiar enough with the justice system to be skeptical about eyewitness testimony, especially when that testimony came from high-school kids who had been drinking at a party late at night. Police, often under pressure from their bosses or the media, sometimes get tunnel vision about making an arrest. It's easy for a police photo identification session to become suggestive or subtly coercive. Some witnesses fear the police, or want to please them, and are easily led or susceptible to influence. Some, particularly friends or family of the victim, rush to identifications to help find and convict the culprit. Other factors, such as intoxication, stress (known as "weapons focus," where a gun is involved), chaos, poor visibility, or faulty memory can very easily cause mistaken identifications. People with similar features can simply be confused with one another. On top of all this, jurors, who are usually unaware of such weaknesses, often treat eyewitness identifications as compelling evidence.

The results can be disastrous, as has been proven conclusively by the recent use of DNA evidence. A study released shortly before Mario's trial, examining the first forty cases where DNA evidence was used to exonerate wrongfully convicted people, found that in *90 percent* of the cases, eyewitness identification had played a major role in the wrongful convictions. In one case, five separate witnesses had mistakenly identified the wrongly convicted defendant. An earlier study of five hundred wrongful convictions concluded that mistaken eyewitness identification had occurred in 60 percent, an astonishingly high number considering that eyewitness identification is an important factor in only 5 percent of criminal trials. At the time of Mario's trial, The Innocence Project, in San Francisco, had recently released a study identifying faulty eyewitness testimony as the "single greatest cause of wrongful convictions nationwide, playing a role in more than 70 percent of convictions overturned through DNA evidence." The United States Supreme Court has recognized that eyewitness identification, particularly in the criminal context, is by its nature fraught with possible error. People with similar features can easily be confused with one another. And yet, in the words of Supreme Court Justice William Brennan, there is "nothing more convincing to a jury than a live human being who takes the stand, points a finger at the defendant and says, 'That's the one!'"

The case against Mario was based on the testimony of one eyewitness, Matthew Padilla. There was no physical evidence that tied him to the crime or that could exonerate him.

Janet sensed there was something wrong with Padilla. During his testimony, he had kept his head down, avoiding eye contact with anyone. His tone and body language told her that he was either lying, scared of something or someone, or far less sure of his testimony than he claimed to be. Padilla had never met Mario before the night of the shooting. How, Janet thought, could he positively identify him based on a glimpse of a few seconds in the dark, from the side, without his glasses, amid all that chaos, with the stress of a gun being fired just a few feet in front of him? She hoped the jury saw what she did.

When the prosecution rested, Janet still thought the evidence against Mario was weak. But even before the defense had presented Mario's case, his attorney had not been particularly impressive.

Anthony Garcia was in his late thirties, five foot five even in his elevated black cowboy boots, with a thick mustache and hair slicked back and gathered in a braided ponytail that extended below his shoulders. During the trial, Garcia spoke softly and tentatively, seemingly intimidated by the judge and the other lawyers. His opening statement had been short and unclear, skipping from argument to argument without any apparent outline or purpose, and the few objections he made during direct examination of the prosecution witnesses were mostly incoherent and were routinely overruled by Judge Jones.

Garcia called only three witnesses in Mario's defense: Gabriel Ramirez, who had driven Mario to the party, and two other friends of Mario's, Candace Avilar and Rosie Aldana. All three testified that they were hanging out with Mario for most of the party in the rear of the backyard, near a blue van.

Gabriel Ramirez testified that when the fight began, Mario was not involved in it, but rather was standing by a keg of beer "picking up on a girl." Rosie Aldana also testified that Mario was not involved in the fight, but had just stepped away from the keg area when the fight happened.

Gabriel testified that when the first shots were fired, Mario was walking toward him and that he saw Mario react to the shots by ducking and then running to join Gabriel, Anthony, Candace, and Rosie, all of whom took cover behind the blue van.

All three witnesses testified to seeing Mario hiding behind the van with them moments after the first shots were fired. And Candace Avilar testified that she specifically noted Mario's location behind the van as the second volley of shots was fired—the shots down the driveway—because Mario was her boyfriend's brother. And all three testified that after waiting behind the van for several minutes after the shooting had stopped, Gabriel Ramirez, Anthony Ramirez, Rosie Aldana, Candace Avilar, and Mario all walked down the driveway and left the party in Gabriel's car.

But because all three witnesses admittedly were friends of Mario's, Bobby Grace easily impeached—discredited—them on cross-examination, for being biased.

Garcia then rested his defense, without calling an eyewitness identification expert to cast doubt on the reliability of Matthew Padilla's identification of Mario, without calling any non-biased witnesses to support Mario's location during the shootings, and without recalling to the stand any of the witnesses who had testified that one of the other defendants had been the driveway shooter.

In his closing argument, prosecutor Grace (apparently realizing that the evidence against Mario was weak) took advantage of the three similar-looking Latino defendants sitting together at the defense table. He painted Mario with the same broad brush by using evidence that had been introduced against Guzman and Rivera:

> There's no getting around or trying to hide the ball on this. The circumstances of this case were gang-related. *Those three* defendants were Highland Park gang members. And this is where the gang evidence comes in with respect to motive and with respect to identification, when you relate it to what *these* gang members or what *these* gang individuals did the night of the party. The fight that occurred, everything that was involved were precipitated by *these* defendants, by their actions. *They* are the ones that injected gang influence or gang overtones into this by hitting people up, by bringing guns...

Sister Janet had to will herself not to jump up and yell, "Objection!" She was furious that Grace was lumping Mario together with the other two as a gang member despite the absence of any evidence whatsoever in the record that he was affiliated with a gang or had been involved in the hitting up or the fight.

She knew that Bobby Grace was a rising star in the District Attorney's Office and that his job was to get convictions. But she felt that this was pushing the ethical boundaries. Where was Garcia, Mario's attorney? Why was he letting Grace get away with this? Still, she felt the jury wouldn't convict Mario on the testimony of Matthew Padilla, the one eyewitness.

The jury deliberated for two days before returning their verdict. Garcia was confident, telling Mario that he was going to walk, no doubt about it, and telling Mario's family that he would be home in a matter of days. As Mario walked into the courtroom that morning, with his hands shackled in front him, he didn't look at the jury, but he kept his head raised.

The courtroom was filled and tense. The family of Martin Aceves, the murder victim, sat on one side, and Mario's family and supporters filled most of the other side. Sister Janet sat in her usual place in the front row, near Virginia Rocha, squeezing her hands together as the jury foreman rose to announce the verdict. She saw Mario's shoulders rise and fall as he let out a deep, quiet breath. In the next few seconds, he would either be set free or taken away to prison for life.

The verdict for Pee Wee came first: guilty on both counts, murder and attempted murder.

Next came Cartoon: guilty on both counts.

"The two men next to me had lost their lives in a matter of seconds, and the cause of their doom was coming my way. 'Not Guilty!' 'Not Guilty!' I prayed," Mario would later write.

The foreman began. "We find the defendant, Mario Rocha..." Mario drew a deep breath and tensed his body.

"Guilty of murder and attempted murder," the foreman read.

There was a stunned silence in the courtroom. Mario exhaled slowly, closed his eyes, and went numb. "I felt spiritually killed, right there," he would say later. As he was escorted out of the courtroom by deputies, his hands cuffed behind him, Mario didn't look back at his mother. It was not an image he wanted to remember.

The sentencing came a few months later. As Mario prepared for court that morning, he wrote in his journal, "Today is the day of my funeral. I wonder who will show up to pay their last respects."

Pee Wee, Cartoon, and Mario, who had just turned eighteen, were all sentenced to two consecutive life terms with no possibility of parole.

"I have been in court for a lot of verdicts and sentencings, but none like that," said Father Kennedy, the priest at Dolores Mission, who knew the Rocha family and attended Mario's trial and sentencing. "You could feel the weight of the cell door slamming shut on him."

Janet was devastated. "I gave God a piece of my mind," she said. "Sometimes when injustice has gone on too long, you just need to tell Him off."

Walking in the church garden one morning, Janet stopped in front of a plaster bust of St. Francis of Assisi. St. Francis was one of her favorite saints. She kept up a running dialogue with him. This time, Janet stood and stared for a long time at the saint who was known for his love of the poor, his generosity, and his simple life. Janet knew that until the age of twenty-six, Francis had been a juvenile delinquent, a wealthy and spoiled kid who robbed and stole for sport.

Janet let him have it. "Francis, you wouldn't be a statue in these gardens today if you had been judged on what you did in *your* youth," she nearly shouted. "They would have put you away for life!"

Janet didn't know what to do. She knew the value that the court system placed on the finality of jury verdicts, even those as egregiously wrong as Mario's. She viewed this as part of "the loyalty to a lie." She knew that even if she could find a competent lawyer to take on Mario's case, overturning a conviction was a million-to-one long shot. She wasn't sure she was strong enough to throw herself into such a cause again, knowing it almost certainly would fail.

As she prayed and thought of little else, Janet received a letter from Calipatria State Prison. It was from Mario. He had written an essay during his bus ride from LA County Jail to a lifetime at the maximum-security state prison in the desert.

> Sitting on this LA County Jail bus, shackled at my waist, wrists and ankles, and wearing my last orange juvie jumpsuit, I gaze through barred and graffiti scarred windows at the beauty I may never again behold. It has been more than two years since I have last seen the outside world, and I fear this may be my final glimpse. Like a soldier going off to war, wondering if he or she will come home again, I wonder if I will make it. Will I survive? Passing through silent cities and peaceful fields, secluded small towns and endless green, yellow, brown hills, everything vanishing too quickly, I stare dead into the eyes of this scared boy on the glass. Grappling for hope through a tunnel of terror I search everywhere until I find, smoldering in the center of this humanity, a stone of black,

> red rage—color that unfolds as you close your eyes to the bright sun when losing the liberty of life as a sixteen-year-old kid; color that evolves into something cancerous, developing and growing inside; the forest of fear blocking one's vision of hope. It is the energy that keeps this brown-eyed boy on the window battling against the fear in the eyes of the young lifer on this bus. Me.*

Reading Mario's letter, Janet realized that the harder question was how could she *not* fight for Mario? She had built her life on faith in a transcendental right that exists regardless of any tallies of wins and losses. Mario was a test of that faith.

"I didn't have a choice," she said later. "God boxed me in."

—ꟾꟾꟾ—

*Excerpted from the forthcoming manuscript by Mario Rocha, *Young Lifer*.

CHAPTER 9

Right to Counsel

LOS ANGELES, DECEMBER 2001

MARIO'S CASE READ like a crime thriller, especially when compared to the hundreds of pages of commercial leases and mezzanine loan guarantees waiting on my desk. It had gangs, guns, murder, and corruption.

Even on my first reading of the trial transcript, something about the case didn't smell right. There were only two shooters. Why had three defendants been prosecuted and convicted of murder? There'd been no charge or jury instruction for aiding and abetting; all three defendants had been convicted of the actual murder. There was not a single shred of evidence that Mario had had anything to do with the shooting of Martin Aceves, the murder victim. The overwhelming evidence pointed to the two other defendants, Guzman and Rivera, as the shooters. They were known, documented Highland Park gang members. Numerous witnesses had seen them accosting people at the party and carrying guns, and had identified them as the two shooters. There was no evidence of a third shooter and no evidence that Mario was a gang member, had been aggressive, was anywhere near the fight, owned a gun, or had a gun at the party.

The trial was a mess. Even the prosecutor appeared not to know who had done what. Some prosecution witnesses identified Guzman as the one who shot and killed Martin Aceves. Others testified that Rivera had shot Aceves. Some identified Guzman as the shooter who fired down the driveway into the fleeing crowd, injuring Anthony Moscato. Others said the driveway shooter was Rivera. One witness, Matthew Padilla, had identified Mario as the driveway shooter. Two others had viewed a police sixteen-pack photo lineup days after the murder and had pointed to Mario as someone "who looks like" the driveway shooter. Even though there was no evidence that Mario was a gang member, the prosecutor, Bobby Grace, had called him one repeatedly in his closing argument. Grace succeeded in blending all three defendants together in the minds of the jury by repeatedly referring to them as "they," "these three gang members," and "the three shooters."

Where was Mario's lawyer? Why hadn't he objected? How had he let this happen?

The second box contained police files and records of their investigation, known as "the murder books." What I found inside was shocking. On February 22, 1996, a week after the murder, the police procured Ramey warrants (warrants that allow the police to bypass the district attorney and go straight to the judge) to arrest Nigel Lobban, Gabriel Ramirez, Anthony Ramirez, and Mario's brother, Danny Rocha, for the murder of Martin Aceves, even though there was not a shred of evidence—

physical, circumstantial, or eyewitness—implicating any of them in the shooting. Nigel Lobban testified at a preliminary hearing and provided a sworn statement that while waving a warrant in his face, the detectives told him he was a suspect in the murder. They threatened to arrest him and get him fired from his job working for a former LAPD officer if he didn't sign a false statement incriminating Mario Rocha. According to Lobban, when he persisted in maintaining that he and Mario were innocent, the officers wrote out a statement and forced him to sign it without giving him a chance to read it. During Lobban's three-hour interrogation in the Hollenbeck police station, he was not read his Miranda rights nor offered a chance to be represented by an attorney.

Gabriel Ramirez, Anthony Ramirez, and Danny Rocha were also brought into the Hollenbeck station and shown, during interrogation, warrants for their arrests for murder.

Later, the investigating officers admitted they knew they lacked "probable cause"—the legal standard for obtaining a warrant—but that they had procured the warrants and detained the targets without formally arresting them in order to "try to obtain a statement" from them, and not because they were suspects.

Worse, potentially, the police had persuaded more than thirty witnesses to sign "witness statement forms" declaring that they did not wish to speak to defense counsel. These forms, though not legally binding, at a minimum encouraged witnesses not to cooperate with the defense.

IT WAS A FASCINATING case, but I didn't know what Latham could do for Mario at this point. He had been tried, convicted, and sentenced, and his conviction, based on the record of the underlying trial, had been upheld on appeal. His attorney's incoherent and bumbling motion for a new trial (literally, the worst piece of writing by a lawyer I had ever seen) had been denied. And what was a murder case doing at Latham in the first place?

I was about to call Bob Long when Steve Newman walked briskly into my office. "I hear you're on Rocha," he said. "Here's a copy of the habeas petition we filed in Superior Court." He tossed onto my desk what looked like a thick legal brief. "Read it to familiarize yourself with the issues. It was just denied, and we've only got three weeks to appeal, so things are going to be intense. I'll have my secretary make a copy of my case file for you."

We? Please tell me you're not...

"There's a seminar tomorrow at the UCLA Law School on habeas corpus," Steve continued. "I need you to go, take notes on everything, collect any materials they hand out, and write up a memo for me by Monday..."

"Hold on a second. I'm supposed to call Bob Long about this," I interrupted, waving the note in my hand and hoping to God that I hadn't signed myself up for another case with Steve.

Steve waved his hand dismissively. "Don't worry about that. Don't bother Bob. I just spoke with him. Bob is the partner on this, but I'm running things day to day."

A string of expletives lodged in my throat. I didn't like Steve or particularly trust him, and the last thing I wanted was to work closely with him for the next three weeks. I thought for a second about backing out of the case then and there. I could easily claim that Greene had just dumped a pile of work on me and

I was too busy on his deal to work on a pro bono case, which was mostly true. Steve could find himself another first-year associate to abuse, and that would be that. But I was intrigued by Mario's case, and I was dying to get away from the document reviews and due diligence, even if it meant working with Steve again.

"Okay," I said. "I'll go."

"One question," I added as Steve was about to leave my office. "How did we get involved in this case?"

Steve smiled crookedly and said, "All roads lead to Sister Janet."

IT WAS LATE IN THE FALL OF 1999 when Sister Janet made her way to the reception area at Latham for her meeting with Bob Long. While she had a good feeling about the meeting, Bob had agreed to meet with her only as a favor to his friend Belinda Walker, a Harvard Law graduate who mentored at-risk youth at the Central Juvenile Hall and happened to be the wife of another Latham senior partner. A week earlier, Belinda had called Bob and told him about a remarkable nun she had met recently. The nun, Sister Janet Harris, had been trying to find a lawyer to represent a young Latino man who had been convicted of murder three years earlier. The nun was sure he was innocent. Belinda told Bob what Janet had told her about Mario and asked if Bob would meet with Janet and at least listen to her story. Perhaps Latham might take the case pro bono.

Bob Long was skeptical. In addition to being a rainmaker bringing in big-fee cases for the firm, he was also one of Latham's hardest-working attorneys, billing close to 3,000 hours a year and spending hundreds more hours serving on the firm's management committees. Meeting with a nun about a convicted murderer *she felt* was innocent was perhaps not the best use of his time, which the firm billed out at more than $500 an hour. But Bob respected Belinda's opinion and judgment, so he agreed to the meeting, "No guarantees," he told her.

Sister Janet and Bob Long met in a small conference room on the sixth floor. Janet was immediately taken with Bob. "I could tell in the first thirty seconds that he was brilliant," she said. "He spoke so intelligently, and he was *so* handsome. He looked like a movie star, like Atticus Finch."

"Thank you for taking this case," Janet began. The presumption was classic Janet, her way of persuading people to do things they might otherwise not want to do. It didn't work as well on a seasoned trial lawyer. Bob explained that he hadn't agreed to anything at this point, but Janet continued as if she hadn't heard him. She laid it on thick, explaining the circumstances of the murder for which Mario had been convicted, describing how she had come to meet Mario in Juvenile Hall, emphasizing what a kind, intelligent person he was. She summarized the travesty of Mario's trial, how the prosecutor had branded him as a gang member on no evidence, and how his attorney had failed him. She explained how she had spoken to kids who had attended the party and others who had told her that Mario was innocent.

"I was ready to get down on my knees and beg if I had to," Janet would later say of her meeting with Long.

Bob admired Sister Janet's passion and dedication to Mario's case and respected her reputation, but he was still skeptical. He was a business lawyer, representing corporations in disputes over money, clients who paid the firm handsomely for his time, not indigent convicts seeking justice. And he wasn't entirely sure how much credibility to give Sister Janet and her conclusions. *She took up this kid's cause because he is a good writer? She knows gang members by their body language?* Perhaps Janet was so emotionally involved in the case that she may have let her emotions cloud her judgment. Even if the facts were as cut and dried as she presented them—and Bob was pretty sure they weren't—overturning a conviction at this stage was almost impossible. Even if this kid *was* innocent, the only avenue left would be some kind of habeas corpus petition, a legal Hail Mary that would take a lot of time, effort, and expense with little chance of success. Bob backed Janet off gently by telling her he would take a look at the transcripts and the case file and let her know.

A few days later, Bob received a letter from the prison at Calipatria. In perfect penmanship, Mario Rocha graciously thanked him for taking on his case, saying that Sister Janet had told him great things about Latham & Watkins and that he looked forward to working with Bob for justice and freedom. Bob smiled at the letter. Sister Janet was playing dirty.

Over the the next few weeks, Bob and Steve Newman read through the papers in the boxes Janet had left with Long, including the transcript of the trial. Bob was pleasantly surprised that, for all her zeal, Janet had not embellished the facts. While it appeared to Bob that the evidence against Mario was weak, what jumped off the pages was the ineptitude of Mario's lawyer. Bob had been lead trial counsel in several big legal malpractice cases in his career. He knew it was hard to show malpractice because the legal standard for competence by lawyers was surprisingly low. But it wasn't impossible. The legal profession does have a bottom-line embarrassment threshold. And to Bob Long, Mario's lawyer had fallen well below that threshold.

But Long had to deal with the practical considerations of asking his firm to take on a case representing a convicted murderer that would surely cost millions of dollars in lost fees and out-of-pocket expenses, would take years, and would have almost no chance of success, all to try to right a single injustice—probably one out of thousands like it. He was not about to do that based solely on a legal technicality of ineffective assistance of counsel. To convince the firm, and himself, that Mario was worth the time, money, and effort, Bob arranged for Mario to take a polygraph.

He passed.

—~—

CHAPTER 10

Denied

A FEW MINUTES AFTER Steve Newman left my office, Adam Greene stormed in. "What's the deal with the edits I sent you to proof?" His eyes were bloodshot, and he looked to be teetering on the verge of a breakdown.

"I got staffed on another case this morning and had some work to do," I told him. "I'm getting started on your stuff now."

Greene's nostrils flared, and his voice went up an octave. "You should not be taking on other work right now! There is more to do on this deal than can possibly be done in the next few months. You need to clear your plate and focus on *this*!" he jabbed his finger into a stack of deal papers for emphasis.

In a sense, he was right. In terms of career advancement at the firm, taking on the pro bono case wasn't a good decision. Greene's IPO was the biggest and most profitable corporate deal going on at the firm. The lead partner on it was Elaine Sherman, the office managing partner. Several other corporate, tax, and real estate partners were working on the deal as well.

Although the low-level associate work wasn't glamorous, it was an opportunity for exposure to a high-stakes deal and to get our names and faces in front of partners. But I already knew I wasn't going to be a corporate lawyer. Pushing paper, dotting *i*'s and crossing *t*'s on corporate deal documents, and boring into the fine print of finance documents and stock option grants wasn't for me. The one drafting session I'd been asked to sit in on, which Greene had called an exciting honor for a junior associate, had consisted mostly of a conference room full of lawyers jousting over semicolons and talking in circles about whether the sub-basement of a building counted in determining whether a building was fifty-four or fifty-five stories high.

I decided to stick to my guns. I thought it might send Greene over the brink if I told him my new case was pro bono. So I only said, "The case is with Bob Long, so there's not much I can do." I put my hands up and shrugged. "Sorry."

STILL GRUMBLING ABOUT having to work with Steve Newman again, I spent four hours that Saturday in a UCLA Law School lecture hall listening and taking notes as two deputy district attorneys explained, in painful detail, the ins and outs of habeas corpus procedure.

Habeas corpus, Latin for "you have the body," one of the most fundamental principles of Anglo-American law, entitles an imprisoned person to challenge in court the legality of their confinement. Habeas corpus is a citizen's ultimate protection against unlawful and arbitrary arrest and detention. It is enshrined in the U.S. Constitution and the constitutions and legal codes of all fifty states. With few exceptions, such as newly discovered DNA evidence, habeas corpus petitions don't second-guess the results of a trial. Instead, they challenge the procedures that led to the conviction—for example, whether an arrest, interrogation, or conduct of a trial met the minimum constitutional guarantee that no person shall be deprived of liberty without due process of law. Habeas corpus is the grounds on which many Guantánamo detainees challenged their arrest and detention without trial or access to legal counsel.

While habeas is a revered legal right, so many habeas corpus petitions are filed that they tend to clog the judicial system. Thousands are filed in state and federal courts every year, most of them handwritten by inmates representing themselves without legal counsel. Although the increasing number of convictions overturned by DNA evidence through habeas proceedings has shined a light on the number of wrongful convictions in the justice system, the hard fact is that a great many habeas petitions make wild and unfounded claims. Courts simply don't have time to read them all carefully. So with the Supreme Court's blessing, the barriers to winning a habeas corpus petition are almost impossibly high. Courts view them with great skepticism. Almost all are thrown out soon after they are filed.

The DAs running the UCLA seminar made that point painfully clear: "The first thing you should make clear to your client, before undertaking any habeas corpus efforts on their behalf, is that this is a long, costly process and they have virtually no shot of winning. You need to make that clear in their mind. *No shot.* There is literally a court clerk who reads—or skims, actually—these habeas petitions with a red 'Denied' stamp poised in one hand. Unless you have exculpatory DNA evidence, there is about a one-in-a-million chance of success on a habeas petition."

From there it got worse.

"Ineffective assistance of counsel is probably the most difficult basis for a habeas claim," the district attorneys agreed. The legal test for ineffective assistance of counsel set by the Supreme Court in the case of *Strickland v. Washington* (known as "the Strickland test") requires a petitioner to prove two things, both by a preponderance of the evidence (meaning "more likely than not"): First, he must prove that his lawyer's performance was "deficient according to prevailing professional norms as they existed at the time of trial." This, the DAs explained, was nearly impossible. "There is a strong presumption of trial counsel's competence at the habeas stage. Lawyers are afforded wide berth for their tactics and 'strategic' decisions at trial. You won't get any sympathy from a judge on this one. Judges were lawyers once, too. They are aware of the difficulties and vagaries of trial practice, and they are skeptical of habeas lawyers picking apart a lawyer's decisions and actions with the benefit of 20/20 hindsight."

And even if the lawyer did screw up, the baseline standard of competence for a lawyer is remarkably low. "Only in the most dramatic and outrageous cases—such as a lawyer sleeping through his client's trial—is any relief going to be given. And even in that case, he must have slept through 'substantial portions' of the trial."

And this "was the easy part." A habeas petitioner must also demonstrate that there is a reasonable probability that *but for the lawyer's incompetence, the result of the trial would have been different.* "Jury verdicts are afforded a strong presumption of reliability, so this amounts to requiring a showing that your client is in fact innocent, although you are not allowed to present direct evidence of your client's innocence unless it is tied to the ineffectiveness-of-counsel claim. It is a mountain to climb."

Wonderful. I had just walked into a case that would take years of work with virtually no chance of success, wouldn't make the firm any money, and would require that I work for Steve Newman, who had been quick to blame me in the past and, if we didn't win, would probably miss no opportunity to blame me again.

I SPENT ALL SUNDAY morning in the office drafting a detailed five-page memo to Steve Newman summarizing the habeas seminar and explaining relevant statutes, cases, procedures, deadlines, and rules. I figured it would give him something to chew on for a while and perhaps keep him off my back for a day or so.

A few minutes later, Newman shot back a two-word response: "Thanks. Helpful." And then another, a few seconds later: "Are you in the office?" I sprang up from my chair, closed and locked my office door from the inside, and turned off my overhead lights. I sat at my desk and waited about ten minutes before responding on my BlackBerry, saying that I had left the office and was almost home in Santa Monica. It was ridiculous to be hiding in my office, playing cat and mouse with Steve, but I needed an afternoon without emails or phones calls giving me "urgent" assignments to do. I wanted to get my bearings on Mario's case, by going piece by piece through the complete case file in the five new boxes Steve had sent to my office, and by rereading the trial transcript and the habeas petition that Latham had submitted and that had recently been denied.

And the more I learned, the more it began to register: I had stumbled into the case of a lifetime.

SOON AFTER MARIO'S arrest, the court had appointed as his defense counsel Katie Trotter, a criminal defense lawyer in private practice who took court-appointed cases for indigent defendants for fees paid by the state. According to the information in the files, Trotter appeared to have begun work on the case immediately and was doing a fine job. She submitted requests to the prosecution that they provide her with contact information for all of the witnesses who had made statements to the police, even those whom the police had persuaded to sign statements saying they didn't want to talk to defense counsel. She drew up subpoenas for twelve key witnesses who she thought might be resistant to testifying.

Trotter represented Mario aggressively at his preliminary hearing, getting Lauro Mendoza to confess that he "wasn't sure" of his identification of Mario, and questioning Matthew Padilla, the key witness against Mario, about his drinking on the night on the party and the fact that he wasn't wearing his prescription glasses.

But not long after the preliminary hearing, a member of Mario's family was approached by Anthony Garcia, who claimed to be an experienced criminal defense lawyer with expertise in murder trials. "He came at us like a used car salesman, promising this and that and saying he could win the case," said Mario's father. The Rocha family, having little understanding of the workings of the justice system and believing that a private attorney would do a better job than a court-appointed one, mortgaged their home to pay Garcia $17,000, in advance, to cover all defense fees and expenses. In fact, at the time Garcia was hired by the Rocha family, his experience was limited to two murder cases, and state bar records indicated that Anthony R. Garcia (same first name, middle initial, and last name) served primarily as court-appointed counsel in juvenile dependency cases in the family court.

After signing up the case and receiving his check from the Rocha family, Garcia had waited more than five months—until less than five weeks before Mario's trial date—to begin his investigation. He did this even though the case was based on eyewitness testimony and even though there were more than fifty potential witnesses to be interviewed, many of whom were juveniles who would be hard to find and get to cooperate. And when Garcia did finally begin, he didn't do much. Although he had requested and received additional money from the court to conduct his investigation, his files contained only *two* witness interview reports from his investigator—out of the fifty or more potential witnesses at the party. Both of the witnesses Garcia's investigator had interviewed were friends of Mario's. They had been easy to find, but were not particularly helpful to the case, and at the trial they would be easily impeached as biased.

The most shocking information came from Garcia's own records of the time he spent working on the case. They showed that in the weeks leading up to trial date, he spent less than eight hours working on the case. I'd spent more time than that getting familiar with the case in my first two days.

It was clear at a glance that Garcia's defense of Mario at trial had been incompetent.

Lauro Mendoza had testified on direct examination by the prosecutor that he caught only a "glimpse" of the side of the face of the person shooting down the driveway toward Anthony Moscato. From that, he had identified Mario out of a sixteen-pack photographic lineup card as a person who "looks like the shooter" he saw. On cross-examination, Garcia failed to highlight the fact that Mendoza had not identified anyone when he was first brought to the police station and shown the lineup cards, but instead, four days later, had suddenly identified Mario. And Garcia failed to bring out on cross-examination the fact that, at the preliminary hearing in July, 1996, Katie Trotter had asked Mendoza, regarding his identification of Mario, "You weren't sure about that were you?" to which Mendoza had answered, "No, I wasn't."

Garcia failed to explore the fact that Bryan Villalobos was the only witness to testify that there were two shooters in the driveway. He failed to point out that Villalobos had positively identified Guzman, not Mario, as the kneeling shooter in the driveway and that this was in direct contradiction to Padilla's and Mendoza's identification of Mario as the kneeling driveway shooter. He failed to point out that Villalobos had said Mario was a person—in a sixteen-pack photo lineup card—who "looks most like" a shooter he claimed to see standing *behind* Guzman (Pee Wee) in the driveway. He failed to explore Villalobos's level of sobriety, in light of his testimony that he had smoked marijuana earlier that evening and every day for the last two or three years.

Matthew Padilla's identification of Mario as the driveway shooter was the only significant testimony against Mario, and Garcia had done nothing to undercut it, even though that would not have been hard. He failed to ask Padilla to give a detailed description of the shooter he claimed to have seen in the dark, for a few seconds, amid the stress of gunfire; failed to ask him to explain why he had testified to hearing twice as many gunshots as every other witness; failed to explore the nature of Padilla's vision problems, even after Padilla testified that "I'm not totally blind, but I do need glasses for reading." And the questions Garcia did ask allowed Padilla to reiterate and emphasize his identification of Mario.

Garcia failed to object when the prosecutor repeatedly referred to Mario as a gang member, despite absence of any evidence in the trial record that Mario was a member of a gang. And he failed to emphasize the fact that there were only two shooters, not three. Amazingly, during his closing argument, his final chance to address the jury, Garcia said explicitly, "With regard to the two shooters, I'm not going to address that."

The more I wrapped my head around the case, the angrier I got. I had been naïve. I'd thought district attorneys were supposed to seek right and fair results, more than track records of convictions. In Mario's case, the DA's office had gone ahead with a prosecution for murder despite no evidence whatever of Mario's involvement in the murder of Martin Aceves, and practically no credible evidence of any involvement by Mario in the "driveway shooting" of Anthony Moscato. They had done their best to bend evidence to paint Mario as a gang member to get a conviction. It was as if Mario were a freebie for them: try two gangbangers for murder and get a third conviction of a Latino kid from the barrio for free!

A FEW DAYS AFTER Mario passed his polygraph test, Latham agreed to represent him. Bob Long believed there was considerable evidence of Garcia's incompetence in the trial record and in Garcia's files of his investigation of the case. What was needed was the second prong of the Strickland test—evidence that Garcia's incompetence would have made a difference in the trial's outcome, that if he had conducted his investigation in a timely manner and conducted the trial responsibly, Mario would have been found not guilty.

Long immediately sought a private investigator to look through the transcripts and police files and to track down and interview as many witnesses as possible. The starting point was to do the investigation that Anthony Garcia had failed to do. Latham hired the private investigative firm of John Brown and Associates, and the case was assigned to a midtwenties investigator and aspiring filmmaker there named Aldo Velasco.

Velasco spent months tracking down almost every witness who had testified at trial and others whose names appeared in the police murder books. Most of them, asking why he wanted to bring up "that stuff" that happened years before, slammed the door in his face. Some said they didn't remember anything. Others told him they were too afraid of gang retaliation to talk to him.

"What I seen I can't say. If my name were just to pop up, forget about it," one of the kids who had attended the party told him. "Not just me, but my family, too. Those fools don't play."

"I felt like there was some other truth out there. Something that people knew but were too scared to say," Aldo later recalled in the documentary film *Mario's Story*.

Frustrated, Aldo decided to start at the beginning. He visited the house on Ebby Street, where the party and shooting had taken place. The home still had the same owners, and they were willing to talk to Aldo. They showed him around and pointed out the bullet hole in the kitchen drywall. They explained that they were out of town during the weekend of the shooting and couldn't be much help. But they gave Aldo the name and contact information of their niece, Laurie Nevarez, who had been staying at the house the weekend of the shooting and had helped organize the party.

Before leaving the home where the murder occurred, Aldo asked the residents his standard questions. "Did any lawyer or investigator ever contact you or interview you about the shooting?"

"No."

"Nobody named Anthony Garcia? No defense lawyers?"

"No."

"If they had, would you have told them what you told me, about Laurie?"

"Sure. Absolutely."

"Thanks very much."

The next day, Aldo contacted Laurie Nevarez by phone. She was now married and living with her husband in Alhambra. She agreed to speak with him, saying she would meet him at the house on Ebby Street that night. Laurie was shy, and nervous about rehashing the details of a painful experience.

Aldo sensed that she felt somewhat responsible for what had happened.

"Tell me what you remember about the party," he said. Laurie explained what Aldo already knew—how her aunt had gone out of town that weekend and Matthew Padilla, the boyfriend of her friend Christina Aragon, had persuaded her to let him throw a party at the house. Padilla took care of getting the beer and liquor and finding the DJ. He strung a tarp up across the driveway at the rear of the house, which acted as a barrier to entry into the backyard. He stood in front of the tarp for most of the night, collecting money from people before admitting them into the party.

"Did you see a fight at some point?"

"Yes, a group of guys started fighting behind the house. Christina and I took a few steps back toward the rear of the yard, and Christina started screaming for Matthew. Matthew came into the back of the yard toward us and stood around for a second trying to stop the fight, when the shots were fired."

"Did you say Matthew Padilla came into the backyard before the first shots were fired?"

"Yes. I saw him. He was walking right toward us."

"Did he stay in the backyard after the first shots were fired?"

"Yes, he was standing around near me and Christina when people were running down the driveway."

"Where was he standing? Can you show me?"

They walked into the backyard and Laurie replayed what she had just told Aldo, pointing out the general area where she had seen Padilla standing when the shots were fired.

"Do you know Mario Rocha?" Aldo asked.

"No. I mean I know he was convicted, but I don't know him personally. I've never talked to him."

"So you would have no reason to say something that wasn't true to help him out?"

"Right."

"One more thing, Laurie. Has anyone ever contacted you or spoken to you from the defense team? Any lawyers or investigators?"

"No. Never."

"If they did, would you have told them what you told me here today?"

"I mean, yes. It's the truth."

After more than four months of getting doors slammed in his face, Aldo had finally gotten his breakthrough: Laurie's statement contradicted Padilla's trial testimony that he was standing in front of the tarp, on the street side, when the first shots were fired. According to Padilla, after hearing the shots, people began fleeing down the driveway, knocking the tarp down. To avoid being trampled, he said he'd stepped to the side, close to the house. From there, he saw the person he later identified as Mario get down on one knee, place a gun in his left hand, and fire down the driveway. But from the area where Laurie placed Padilla when the shots were fired, on the backyard side of the tarp, he would have been in no position to identify the driveway shooter. He would, at best, have seen only the back of his head.

Laurie also provided Aldo with the contact information of Christina Aragon, Padilla's girlfriend at the time of the party, who was standing with Laurie in the back of the yard. When

Aldo contacted Christina, she echoed what Laurie had told him. She had called for Padilla during the fight. He had come into the backyard before the shots were fired and remained there until the shooting stopped. She, too, had never been contacted by Garcia or his investigator.

While this did not directly prove that Mario was innocent, it undercut the testimony of the only witness who had identified him as a shooter with any degree of reliability. Laurie Nevarez and Christina Aragon had no reason to lie to help Mario. Garcia had never contacted them, and if he had, they would have told him what they knew and would have testified at trial.

A few months later, on October, 20, 2000, Steve Newman and Bob Long filed a motion for habeas corpus in Los Angeles Superior Court, arguing that Mario had received ineffective assistance of counsel based on Garcia's failure to conduct a timely and adequate investigation of the case, his failure to seek a separate trial for Mario, his many shortcomings at trial, and that Garcia's incompetence had made a difference in the outcome.

Their petition was assigned to Judge Larry Fidler, where it sat for more than a year and a half before it was returned with a one-word ruling:

DENIED.

CHAPTER 11

You're Going to Save His Life

LOS ANGELES, JUNE–DECEMBER 2002

"YOU CAN'T DO THAT!" Steve Newman screamed at me. He stomped his feet and waved his arms in exasperation. How could he have been stuck working with a monumental idiot like me? In a memo about some research for our new habeas petition, I had cited cases using the standard blue book legal citation form.

"In the California courts, you cite according to the California rule!" Steve said. "The goddamn date goes after the goddamn case name, not at the end. Christ! This is basic stuff!"

I felt about two feet tall. "Sorry Steve," I said, trying to calm him down. "I didn't know. I won't do it again."

It was only later that I found out that California courts accept cases cited either way and that the "California rule" method was only Steve's personal preference.

For the next three weeks, I found myself being pulled apart and swatted back and forth like a dead fish between two cats:

Adam Greene and Steve Newman. Greene insisted that his IPO deal took priority, frantically tossing assignments at Wilke, Davies, and me, insisting that we clear our schedules and pull frequent all-nighters inputting changes into his IPO prospectus.

But Greene was a teddy bear compared to Steve Newman. Like Greene, he seemed to live at the office. He fired off emails at all hours, seven days a week, asking me to find cases supporting the arguments in our habeas petition and assigning me portions of the petition to draft. Moody and intense, he had no patience for my other workload or my lack of experience. "Don't give me that. Everyone here is busy. If you can't get this done, I'll find somebody else!" he would bark. When I made the mistake of stopping by his office to ask a question about something, he threw a fit. "It's not my job to answer your questions. It's your job to answer mine!" When I sent him a section of the appeal I had written that I thought was pretty good, he sent it back the next day with one word scrawled across the top in red ink: "Yuck!"

But over the weeks, as our habeas petition to the Court of Appeal began to take shape, for the first time I saw the case—the facts, legal arguments, and analysis—as a whole. And the client as a real person whose life was at stake. I began to understand that this case was about correcting an injustice, not about fulfilling an assignment and not just an interesting diversion from document review. And I began to develop a grudging respect for Steve Newman.

I had begun Mario's case thinking that Steve's short temper, incessant demands, and zero-tolerance perfectionism were simply the result of him being a prick who derived sadistic enjoyment from belittling junior associates. I figured he was working on the case only as a way to suck up to Bob Long. But I came to see there was more to him. Steve was an eighth-year associate, up for partner at the end of the year, and he was juggling a lot of other billable cases that were far more important to his career and partnership prospects. Other associates in his position would have considered Mario's case, while exciting and noble, as a nuisance and a loser. Steve didn't have to be working this hard on it. With a lot less effort and stress, he could have put together a good habeas petition that covered the facts and necessary arguments, and nobody would have known the difference. This was a habeas corpus petition, after all. We were expected to lose.

But good wasn't good enough for Steve. For all his bluster, I could see that he cared about this case, and about Mario, and he had his own standards. He knew the odds we were up against, and he wanted our appeal to be airtight, powerful, overwhelming. He demanded perfection because perfection was the only thing that would give us a chance. He organized the massive amounts of legal research and evidence, and he wrote persuasively. He did all this while working as lead counsel or second chair on a handful of billable cases that could make or break his chance to become a partner. Maybe he could stand to lighten up a bit, but I was learning a lot from him.

We had almost finished the habeas petition to the Court of Appeal when something caught my eye: In his statement to the police shortly after the shooting, at the preliminary hearing, and at trial, Matthew Padilla had described the shooter as "getting down on his right knee, placing the gun in his left hand," and firing down the driveway. In each instance it was the same: right knee, left hand. When I brought this to Steve's attention, his eyes got wide. He immediately called Mario's mother, Virginia, who confirmed that Mario was right-handed. "Great work!" he said. "Let's add a section to the petition pointing out that Garcia never even noticed that Padilla had identified a left-handed shooter. We'll get a declaration from Virginia saying that Mario is right-handed."

When we finished the petition, I was surprised by how good it was. It laid out clearly how Anthony Garcia had failed to conduct an adequate investigation of the case and had failed Mario at trial. It argued persuasively, using declarations signed under penalty of perjury from witnesses Laurie Nevarez and Christina Aragon, that if Garcia had gone to the crime scene and talked to the owners of the house, he would have found witnesses able to undercut Matthew Padilla's identification of Mario.

Unlike some partners, who insisted on rounds of heavy editing on every brief, costing the client more billable hours while often resulting in few important changes, Bob Long made only a few minor edits to our appeal, moving a few paragraphs and changing a word or phrase here and there. Each of his edits made the writing crisper and the arguments more compelling. He sent an email to Steve and me commending us and calling the appeal "a powerful piece of work." It was gratifying to get praise from a senior partner like Bob, and I was proud of the work Steve and I had done, but still I figured it was all for nothing. The words of those district attorneys at the UCLA seminar kept playing in my head: "You have no shot."

ON THE MORNING the petition was to be filed, I arrived early and headed over to our "war room"—the fortieth-floor conference room we had commandeered for Mario's case—for one last check that the petition and exhibits were in order. Two strides into the room, I stopped short. At the opposite end of the long conference table stood four women huddled around the petition, holding hands with their heads bowed. Three were middle-aged and Hispanic. The fourth, who looked to be in her sixties, was a small white woman with short white hair and a cross hanging from her neck. She whispered a blessing as the three Hispanic women slowly waved their hands over the petition. I glanced at Steve, who was sitting in a chair at the near end of the conference table casually observing the ritual. "Can't hurt," he said with a shrug.

When the blessing was finished, Steve introduced me to Mario's mother, Virginia Rocha, and his two aunts, Bertha and Martha. Virginia and Martha gave me a long hug and thanked me for helping Mario.

Mario's aunt Bertha looked concerned. "How old are you?" she asked.

"Twenty-eight," I told her.

"Mario is twenty-four, she said quickly. You are almost the same age." She looked at Steve. "Steve, he looks too young to be a lawyer. He is working on Mario's case?"

"Don't worry, Bertha," Steve said, seemingly accustomed to dealing with Bertha's concerns. "Ian is helping out, but I am still in charge."

Martha apologized to me and quietly scolded her sister. But I wasn't offended. Mario and his family had been burned badly by an incompetent attorney, and they had every right to be wary of someone new who looked too young for the job. If Mario were my relative, I wouldn't want me as his lawyer either.

After the petition and exhibits had been taken away to be filed, I was about to leave the conference room when the slight, elderly white woman who had offered the blessing stopped me. She clasped my hand between hers and looked me squarely in the eye for a few seconds.

"You must be Ian," she said calmly. "Steve has told me so much about you. Thank you for all you've done for Mario."

Steve was standing nearby shaking his head as if to say, "Don't feel special, she does this to everyone."

"I'm Janet," she said, still holding my hand in hers.

"Oh, right! You're the one who brought us the case. NICE... TO...MEET YOU!" I replied, as if she were hard of hearing.

She smiled and graciously ignored my slight. "I may have brought it here, but you are the ones who are walking on water. You are the ones doing God's work."

She stared at me silently for another moment and then said matter-of-factly, "You are going to save his life. I know it."

My first impression of Sister Janet Harris was that she was a sweet old lady who was possibly out of her mind. *God's work?* I bet that's the first time anyone had described what goes on in a Latham conference room that way. *Save his life?* Thanks for the blessing and all, Sister, but hasn't anyone told you that this is a habeas corpus petition, and therefore is bound to lose? But even in this brief meeting, Sister Janet's confidence and the strength of her convictions were contagious. She had a kind of magic about her, and I instantly liked her and wanted to please her.

MONTHS PASSED WHILE our petition languished in the Court of Appeal. Adam Greene's IPO deal kept me busy most days, but because I had taken "time off" (Greene's words) to work on Mario's case, I was less involved in the IPO than my friends Mike Wilke and Jon Davies, who were working around the clock seven days a week, with no end in sight. Greene's work was manageable enough, and it allowed me to take on a few other cases. I was sent for two weeks of document review to Manchester, England, where I sat in a dusty warehouse all day and night with a handful of other first-years, only to find that the case had settled and our work had been for nothing. I researched and wrote a brief on behalf of a developer in a dispute with the plumbers' union, arguing that "no-flow" urinals fit within the municipal code's definition of "low-flow" urinals.

And I was assigned to work on another healthcare fraud case, with a partner named John Oliver. This time, however, instead of just reviewing documents (although I did that, too), I spent weeks at the client's office taking notes while Oliver, a former federal prosecutor, methodically interviewed hospital employees about their complex Medicare billing systems and procedures—"Tell me again how the front-end billing software system creates the TSI report assigning Medicare codes to various patients?"—sometimes for twelve hours at a time. I downed pots of coffee and tried to stay awake.

Observing Oliver engage in torturously complex and often repetitive questioning over even the smallest details of the hospital's billing process, I realized what my trial advocacy professor in law school had meant when he said, "Litigation is bathtub learning." Litigators have to become quick-study experts in the subjects of their cases, learning in a few days or weeks minute and complex details that experts in the topic spend years mastering. After they've filled their brains and the case is done, they then pull the plug and make room for the next case.

Maybe it's the long hours and bathtub learning year after year that make a lot of litigators seem a little odd to the rest of the world. There is so much material to understand and so many moving parts rattling around in the brain that things such as social norms and routine pleasantness get pushed aside as "unimportant facts." Oliver, for example, while reputed to be a brilliant litigator, seemed uncomfortable with or uninterested in any sort of basic human interaction. He ignored routine pleasantries such as handshakes, invaded other people's personal space, and questioned the hospital employees in a robotic, expressionless monotone, inching closer to them as he talked, for hours on end, day after day. In the two weeks I worked closely with him, not once did he show any sign of a personality. When we met in his office to discuss the interviews, he would pull his chair so close to mine that our knees had to be positioned uncomfortably so as not to touch. After I mumbled my thoughts about the interviews, he would stare at me blankly for an awkwardly long time, unleash a shrill noise from somewhere near his throat, and continue staring.

THE SHOCK I INITIALLY felt at the long hours and boredom of the work had subsided a bit and been replaced mostly by apathy. Still, while I figured a lot of people worked at jobs they didn't like, most didn't make nearly as much money as I did. For the next few months my billable work remained pretty much the same, but I was getting more comfortable with it. I was a master of document reviews, I was becoming handy with Westlaw and Lexis research, and I could whip out a basic legal memo pretty quickly. My first two semiannual reviews by the Associates Committee came and went without incident. Both were conducted in my office by a senior associate on the Committee, who read what the attorneys I'd worked for had said about me. They all gave me high marks for teamwork and attention to detail and wrote that I was working at or above the level expected. I was pleasantly surprised to discover that my best review had come from Adam Greene, who gave me fives and five-pluses (out of five) across the board and added that I was a team player who had pitched in on several all-nighters—which made me want to take back every evil thought I'd ever had about him. My worst review came from Steve Newman, who gave me mostly threes and fours. I had heard that the committee considered a single three on any review a red flag, but when I asked the interviewer about it, she laughed. "Generally speaking, that's right, but everyone knows that Steve is tough. A three from him is actually not that bad." Later, I would hear that Steve had given another first-year associate ones across the board, and she had later left the firm.

Others had endured enough. After spending a weekend doing emergency document review, my roommate Matt burst through the door to our apartment late on Sunday night, dropped his bags, and announced, "I can't take this anymore. This fucking place is not going to be on my tombstone! I'd rather live in a cardboard box under the freeway for the rest of my life than spend another Saturday night reviewing documents." A few weeks later, he got a job as a legislative assistant to a United States congressman and was gone. He was the sixth member of my class to leave in the first year.

I hadn't even started looking for a new place to live when, driving through the Santa Monica Canyon on the way back to my apartment after a rare few hours of surfing at the beach, I spotted a "For Sale" sign in front of a small house. On a whim, I decided to take a look. The house was a two-bedroom, one-bath midcentury California bungalow with a small courtyard in the front, a brick patio and outdoor fireplace in back, and a price tag in the middle six figures. It had a few quirks, such as the washer and dryer being in a shed on the patio and forest green paint on every surface, inside and out. But otherwise it was perfect: it was two blocks from the beach, and it sat between the "Santa Monica Stairs," two long sets of stairs running up the canyon hillside with a constant stream of LA's beautiful people marching up and down them with their personal trainers. "It's a steal," the real estate agent told me. "It'll double in three years!"

I'd never given much thought to buying a house and didn't think I could afford one. But when I called the bank to get information about a mortgage, as soon as I told them I was an attorney at Latham, they almost fell over themselves to loan me money. That was it. At twenty-eight, I owned a home in one of the wealthiest zip codes in the country. I was too busy and too caught up in my new home and the other trappings of a Latham income to realize that the golden handcuffs had just become tighter.

—∾—

CHAPTER 12

You'll Do Fine

LOS ANGELES, DECEMBER 2002

IT HAD BEEN four months since we'd filed our habeas corpus petition to the Court of Appeal, when Steve Newman walked into my office on a Friday afternoon triumphantly waving a piece of paper.

"We got it!" he announced proudly. "We're going to get a hearing!"

I had never seen Steve so pleased. The Court of Appeal had ordered the State of California to provide a formal written response to our petition and had ordered that a hearing take place in the Superior Court before a judge other than Judge Fidler, the judge who had held our last petition for a year and a half before denying it. What the Court of Appeal was now requiring was an evidentiary hearing—a sort of mini-trial—to determine if we could prove the allegations in our habeas petition: that Mario had received ineffective assistance of counsel at his trial and that his lawyer's incompetence had contributed materially to his conviction. If we could prove those two things—if we could win at the evidentiary hearing—Mario would get a new trial.

WINNING AT THE evidentiary hearing was still a long shot. But it was no longer a "no shot." "We've climbed the first mountain!" Steve shouted.

That Sunday morning in Highland Park, Father Michael Kennedy invited members of his mostly Latino congregation at the Dolores Mission Catholic Church to come forward, say a few words, and receive a special prayer. This was not unusual at LA churches. At some, parishioners asked for prayers to help heal a sick pet or calm their anxiety over getting a child into the college of his or her choice. At the Dolores Mission, Father Kennedy asked the mothers with incarcerated sons to come forward so that his congregation could pray for them. The filmmakers of *Mario's Story* captured a long line of worried-looking women who approached the front of the modest church and, one by one, spoke the name of a son and the prison where he was being held. After each, Father Kennedy led the congregation: *"Oiganos, Señor"* ("Hear us, O Lord").

Virginia Rocha was last in line, and by the time her turn came she was almost in tears. *"Por mi hijo Mario Rocha, que esta en Calipatria..."* Virginia trailed off as the congregation murmured its prayers and Father Kennedy added in conclusion, *"Pidiendo a la Virgin de Guadaloupe que les protegen sus hijos como las madres que sufren y lloren con sus propios hijos, les benedigan este Domingo"* ("Praying that the Virgin of Guadalupe protects her sons and the mothers who suffer and cry over their sons, bless them this

Sunday"). Father Kennedy paused as Virginia returned to her seat, and then he continued in Spanish: "We have some good news for those who know Virginia, Mario's mother... Her son just received news that they have agreed to hear his case—how do you say—'on appeal.' Less than 1 percent of cases like this are accepted. So it's very good news and let's give a big round of applause to Mario's mother." The congregation burst into applause and well-wishers patted Virginia on the shoulder as she wiped tears of joy from her eyes. Sister Janet sat beaming beside her.

That afternoon, the Rocha family—cousins, aunts, uncles, nieces, nephews—gathered for a celebration that lasted well into the evening. Food and drink were plentiful, and spirits were high. At one point, as the children played in the backyard, the rest of the family gathered in the cramped living room to listen to David, Mario's cousin and close friend, ceremoniously read the Court of Appeal's order:

"On Habeas Corpus, good cause showing, therefore, the People of the State of California are hereby ordered to show cause in the matter of In Re Mario Rocha..."

David explained the significance of the legalese. "This means he's going to get a hearing! They say this is like finding a needle in a haystack. This almost never happens!" The family then stood in a circle holding hands and prayed, led by Mario's maternal grandmother, the matriarch of the family.

ON MONDAY, I WAS in the war room eagerly organizing the files for Mario's case when Steve walked in. He was moving slowly, which was unusual for him, and his head slumped down to his shoulders. He didn't say anything as he sank into a chair across the conference room table from me. We sat there in awkward silence for a moment.

"Something wrong?" I finally asked.

"I'm leaving the firm," he said without looking up.

"What!?" For a second I thought he was kidding, but the look on his face told me this wasn't a joke. "Why?"

It didn't look as if the firm would be making any litigation partners in LA, and he had been encouraged to move to the New York office for a better shot.

I didn't know how to respond. Steve and I weren't exactly friends, but I could see how hard this was for him. I'd heard that it was becoming more and more difficult for associates to make partner these days. "It used to be that if you worked hard, billed your hours, did great work, and paid your dues for eight years, you made partner," a mid-level associate I was friendly with explained to me. "Now the partners who made partner in those days don't want to share the equity pot of gold unless they absolutely have to. The new standard for making partner is 'Can the firm live without you?' and the answer is invariably yes." Still, how could they risk losing Steve? He lived for the firm. He billed 2,500 hours a year. And he was a great lawyer.

"That's crazy, Steve. I'm sorry." And I was. He was a pain to work for, but I respected, even admired, his skill and dedication as a lawyer. "What are you going to do?"

"I've got a house here, a new baby. I'm not moving. I've already got an offer to be a partner at another firm. I'm taking it."

We sat in silence for another minute. Finally, he lifted his head and looked at me for the first time.

"So, do you think you're ready?"

"Ready for what?"

"Ready to take over the case—Mario's case."

I shot a panicked glance at him. I was a first-year whose legal experience up to that point consisted primarily of reviewing documents. Yes, I had been working part-time on Mario's case for *six months*, but I had been mostly in the back rooms doing research and writing drafts for Steve. I didn't know the supervising partner, Bob Long, I didn't know Mario, and I had never written a final draft ready for filing. The idea that I could competently take over for a hard-charging eighth-year associate on a life-and-death case heading for trial was nuts. But it was too late. Steve waved a hand at me dismissively.

"You'll do fine. I told Bob I thought you could handle it," he said.

"*Christ,* Steve. What did Bob say?"

"He's not very happy. But…"

"No shit he's not happy! I'm a first-year associate. I've never even met him." Another dismissive wave from Steve.

"If you commit to it, you'll be fine. But there is going to be a ton of work to do to get ready for the hearing. It might take 50 percent of your time over the next year."

"Is that okay? Am I going to get in trouble for spending that much time on a pro bono case?"

"Not if you win."

"And if we lose?"

A smile crept across Steve's face.

"Then you can come see me for a job."

—~—

CHAPTER 13

Nice to Meet You

LOS ANGELES, CALIPATRIA, JANUARY 2003

MY SECRETARY, DEBBIE, scrambled from her desk and hustled to intercept me in the hallway outside my office.

"Where have you been?" she asked nervously.

"Lunch, why?"

"Your phone has been ringing off the hook. I let the first few go to voicemail but..." She paused to consult her notes. "In the past five minutes, a woman named Sister Janet called and she sounded pretty upset."

"Okay."

"A reporter from the *Daily Journal* called. Said she has been following the Rocha case and wants to speak with you."

"Strange, but okay."

"And *Bob Long* just called. He wants you to call him ASAP."

I felt my stomach tighten. "Thanks," I mumbled, and scurried into my office.

It had been only a little more than an hour since my conversation with Steve Newman. My head was still spinning. I had figured I would be hearing from Bob Long soon, but I'd hoped to have some time to put my thoughts together. After my initial shock at the news of Steve's departure, I realized this was an opportunity for me. It was a chance to have a real role on an interesting case that was heading for trial. A chance to be involved in higher-level legal work—trial preparation and strategy—and to work directly with a senior partner, without Steve Newman barking in my ear constantly. The only remaining hurdle was to convince Bob Long that I was up to the task, that he could trust me to handle the work and responsibility of being the lead associate on the case.

I took a deep breath and dialed Long's extension.

"Bob Long," he answered.

"Bob, hi, it's Ian Graham. Sorry I missed your call, I was just out grabbing lunch and..."

"No problem. Good to speak with you finally. Listen, I think it's about time we met."

Among the floors at Latham, the forty-fourth had by far the highest concentration of heavy-hitter partners. As I circled the floor, I passed the offices of Teddy McMillan, a senior partner in the Litigation Department; Elaine Sherman, the LA office managing partner; and Stanton Pell, the Corporate Department's biggest rainmaker who, I'd heard, is chauffeured to work every day so he can start billing even before he walks in the door. Finally, I spotted Long's office. His door was open, but I knocked anyway.

"Hey there! Come on in," he said, standing up to shake my hand. "Good to finally put a face with the name." Bob was disarmingly friendly. And tall—six-three, I guessed. He seemed so relaxed and good-natured that I couldn't help wonder, *what's the catch?*

His office was huge and well kept. On his large oak desk were well-organized stacks of deposition transcripts and legal briefs. A round oak table with a few chairs stood in one corner, next to matching built-in cabinets. Degrees, awards, and artwork hung on the walls, and among the bookshelves behind his desk were pictures of his wife and sons and framed press clippings from a few of his major trial victories.

"Have a seat," he said, motioning to a chair across from his desk. I noticed a copy of my résumé sitting in his in-box.

"First of all, I want to thank you for all the work you've done on this case," Bob began. "That brief you put together with Steve was a powerful piece of work."

"Thanks." Whatever displeasure he felt about Steve Newman's departure, apparently he wasn't intending to take it out on me.

He looked at me for a few seconds. "So, what else are you working on these days?"

I responded instinctively, trying to sound busy, the way associates do when asked that question by partners.

"I'm on the Wolf Partners IPO, so that's keeping me pretty busy. I'm doing a diligence project, and..."

I thought I was sounding pretty good, but Bob's face suddenly contorted as if I had emitted a foul odor.

"You're Corporate?" he asked.

"No, no," I said, realizing my mistake. At the bottom level, associate work, whether corporate or litigation, is pretty much the same: "Look at these documents and take notes." But up a little higher, the delineation is clear and important. Corporate associates are familiar with deal documents and the legal issues they involve. Litigation associates know the rules of civil procedure, the various stages of litigation and corresponding motions to be drafted and filed. I had essentially just admitted to Bob that I didn't know a complaint from a hole in the ground. "That's just what I've been assigned so far," I sputtered, trying to cover myself. "I'm also working on a healthcare case with John Oliver and have done a few other litigation assignments. I want to do litigation and I plan on joining the department after next year."

"Well, good," he said firmly. "To tell you the truth, I've got no idea what those corporate lawyers do all day. I think we've got something here considerably more interesting to do than looking at documents."

He took a deep breath and leaned back in his chair. "I suppose you've heard about Steve?"

"Yes, he told me this morning. It's too bad."

Bob's face contorted again. "Well, that's his business, I suppose," he muttered. "We've certainly got our work cut out for us on this case. The first thing I think we need to look into is the process we're dealing with. What happens next? What kind of schedule are we looking at? What are the rules governing an evidentiary hearing? What is the framework here?"

I was busy scribbling his instructions on my legal pad when I realized, *hey, I already know this stuff.* This was my chance to make a good impression.

"I've done some work on this already," I interrupted. "The

DA's office has sixty days to file their response to our brief, called a 'return,' I believe. We then have sixty days to respond to the return. After that, the hearing will be scheduled. Although the underlying case is criminal, the hearing is a civil proceeding, and the rules of evidence apply. We can present witnesses, and we have to prove our case by a preponderance of the evidence. There is no jury, just the judge."

Long didn't say anything for a moment, but I took it as a good sign that he didn't make a face.

"Well, we're not just going to sit on our butts waiting for the DA's response," he said. "I need to get myself up to speed on this case. It would be helpful if you could put together a chronology of all the relevant events in this case for me, and start making witness binders for every witness who testified at the trial, including their testimony and any other statements they made to police, investigators, or anyone."

"Sure," I said. "I'll get right on it. Anything else?"

He thought for a moment. "Yes. I think you should pay Mario a visit as soon as possible. Introduce yourself, and explain to him what you just told me about the process going forward so he knows what to expect."

"Okay. Will do."

"Just be careful to manage his expectations. I'm guessing he's pretty jazzed about all of this. He needs to understand that the odds are still quite long here."

CALIPATRIA IS A 230-mile drive from Los Angeles, as far away as one can get and still be in Southern California. The state prison's litigation coordinator had told me I could meet with

Mario from one to two o'clock on a Wednesday afternoon. Considering that I would be hitting the LA rush-hour traffic on the way back, it would definitely be an all-day trip, which was a disaster. Adam Greene's IPO was finally inching toward closing, and he had issued an "all hands on deck" call for that week. Mike Wilke, Jon Davies, and I were supposed to be across the street at the printer 24/7, ready to make sure any last-minute changes to the prospectus were made, proofread, and included correctly in the final printed version.

I broke the news to Greene on Monday, two days before my trip to Calipatria. Luckily, when I told him I needed to be out of the office on Wednesday "to meet with a client," he was screaming at someone on a conference call and was too busy to argue. He rolled his eyes, pressed the mute button on his phone, and offered me a deal: "If you can give me an all-nighter tonight through tomorrow, and all night Thursday, then fine."

"Deal," I said.

The night before my trip to meet Mario, I slept fitfully, even though I had pulled an all-nighter and then worked until midnight. I'd never been to a prison, let alone a super-max out in the desert; and I'd never talked to an inmate, let alone a lifer. By all accounts, Mario was bright and courteous. His only chance for freedom was now largely in my hands. Would he trust me? Could we bridge the differences in our backgrounds and experiences? How awkward would it be, really?

After the prison guards guided me through the security procedures, I first met Mario in the large cafeteria-like room at the Calipatria prison that is used for family visits on weekends. It was a Wednesday and there were no other attorneys visiting, so we had the room to ourselves. Mario sat waiting on a plastic chair at a table in the center of the room when I arrived. Six feet tall and powerfully built, with black-rimmed glasses, a thin moustache, and a shaved head, he was leaner, less pudgy, and more adult-looking than in his pictures. He was dressed in a blue prison jumpsuit and was unshackled. He stood and looked me in the eye.

"Nice to meet you, Ian," he said politely.

I was nervous. Among other firsts, Mario was the first *client* I had ever met, and I wanted to make a good impression. Steve had told me that Mario liked to read the case opinions we cited as legal authority in his habeas petitions, so I had brought with me copies of all the cases included in the last petition. Mario accepted them graciously, and then said with a smile that he had already read most of them.

Whatever Mario thought of me, I was quickly impressed by him. As I explained the Strickland standard for ineffective assistance of counsel that we would have to satisfy, and the procedures and rules for the hearing, I thought I might be getting too technical and that maybe I was talking over his head. This wasn't easy stuff for anyone to understand. But Mario followed it easily, picking up complex legal concepts, peppering me with on-point questions about different elements of our case, and offering perceptive strategy suggestions for the upcoming hearing. He was obviously very bright, articulate, and steady.

Our allotted hour was almost over when I came to the final item on my list. While I was reviewing the police "Murder Book," a statement one witness had given to the police had jumped out at me. This witness had told the police that he had seen *three*

Highland Park gang members involved in the fight: Mario's two co-defendants, Guzman (Pee Wee) and Rivera (Cartoon) and a third man the witness identified by his gang moniker, "Joker." This was a strong piece of evidence. If there had been three gang members involved in the shootings—the prosecution's claim and the basis for Mario's conviction—then the third shooter was more likely to have been Joker than Mario. But, curiously, the police had not done any follow-up investigation of the witness's statement and had made no effort to investigate Joker's involvement. Everyone—police, witness Matthew Padilla, the DA's office, prosecutor Bobby Grace, and the jury—had focused instead on Mario as the phantom third shooter.

When I asked Mario if he knew a Highland Park gang member called Joker, he paused and his expression grew serious. Then he leaned forward and whispered.

"Yes, I know Joker, and I know why you are asking. But he is in here with me, and you can't bring his name into this case. He is *connected*."

I didn't know exactly what Mario meant by "connected," but I had heard stories about prison gangs, and the tone of Mario's voice told me I should drop it and move on, which I did—for the time being.

Cruising back to Santa Monica, with the sun setting to my left, I felt our meeting had gone well. Mario had made a big impression on me. I was about his age, but in every other way our lives could hardly have been more different. I had arrived at Latham, the big, prestigious law firm, from an affluent neighborhood in Washington, D.C., an elite Quaker high school, Rice University on a baseball scholarship, and the University of Texas Law School, from which, thanks to my parents, I had graduated debt-free. I had pursued a career motivated solely by money, and never given much thought to broader issues of social justice. Mario was at least as bright as I was, very possibly more so. His heart was generous, his interests were wide, and his gift for writing was formidable. But he had grown up in the LA barrio, without the opportunities, benefits, and second chances of a privileged upbringing. I wondered how I would have fared growing up in his world, and he in mine.

I felt blindsided. Until now I'd been too busy to think about the emotional side of meeting Mario. Now suddenly his case was no longer merely about arguments on paper, but about a real person, who was depending on me, whose loss of freedom I had seen firsthand. These thoughts turned over in my head as I blasted the air-conditioning to stay awake on the four-hour drive back through the California desert.

CHAPTER 14

These Deficiencies Have Cost Me

LOS ANGELES, JANUARY–OCTOBER 2003

WITH THE BEGINNING of 2003, I officially became a second-year associate. Along with the rest of my associate class, I'd just received a $20,000 lockstep raise in salary, apart from any year-end bonus. And remarkably, there was now an entire class of first-year associates wandering around the office with even less legal experience than I had. They were recognizable by their eager faces and enthusiastic attitudes. I'd made it a full year with no visible signs of damage, other than the Gucci loafers and a slowly creeping waistline. Eight members of my incoming associate class—one-sixth of those who started in LA—had left the firm, five during the first year, and three immediately after year-end bonuses were handed out.

After the excitement and emotion of Mario's case, it was hard to settle down to billable work again. But I needed to do that. The DA's office got two extensions for filing their return, so it would be months before we would have to answer it. A new annual tally of billable hours had begun on January 1, and I knew I needed to rack up a lot of billable work to offset the unbillable time I would spend on Mario's case when it started up again.

It wasn't all drudgery. One of the first activities of the new year for the second-year associates was a mandatory weekend in the office for deposition training. A deposition, in a nutshell, consists of formally questioning a potential witness under oath, prior to a trial. It is held out of court, usually in a law firm's conference room, with no judge present. Depositions are taken to preserve evidence, find out what a witness would say if examined during the trial, and pin the witnesses down so they cannot spring a surprise by changing their testimony at trial. The lawyer taking the deposition asks the witness questions, a court reporter makes a transcript, and in most cases, the proceeding is video-recorded. Depositions are a key element of the fact-finding, or discovery, period of a lawsuit. Done well, they can sometimes lay the foundation for a motion for summary judgment or a favorable settlement. If the witness is unavailable at trial, the deposition video can be used as testimony.

The training began on Friday afternoon with a videotape of a Latham partner taking a deposition. This particular video apparently was selected to get us in the mood, as it contained an example of every litigator's dream: catching the witness in a lie.

The witness was a young hotshot executive who was not happy about some lawyer taking up his day with plodding questions. He was getting testy. A key point in the case was whether this witness wrote or read a particular email that had turned up in evidence with all the names blacked out. The Latham partner had already asked him about it once, earlier in the deposition, and the witness denied knowing anything about it. Now, hours later, with the witness tiring, the partner was circling back. The conversation went something like this:

PARTNER: I'd like you to look again at what's been previously marked Defendant's Exhibit 2.

WITNESS: [agitated] Again? I thought we went through this already?

PARTNER: [calmly] If you would, please.

WITNESS: Okay. Now what?

PARTNER: You stated before that you are certain you never saw this email or were aware of its contents, is that correct?

WITNESS: Yes.

PARTNER: Drawing your attention to the two handwritten comments on the page, can you read those for the record please?

WITNESS: [rolling eyes] The third sentence of the second paragraph is circled and the comment reads, "Quite a stretch." The last sentence of paragraph three is circled and the comment reads, again, "Quite a stretch."

PARTNER: Did you write those "Quite a stretch" comments on this email?

WITNESS: No.

PARTNER: Understanding that this email, as you have previously testified, contains information relating directly to your duties for Company X and that, again, as you testified, you would in the usual course of business read and review a communication such as this, how can you be sure that these "Quite a stretch" comments are not yours?

WITNESS: [with visible agitation] Because that just isn't a term I use, "Quite a stretch." I don't think I've ever used that expression; it's just not something I say.

PARTNER: Is that the only reason you are sure these comments are not yours?

WITNESS: I suppose so, yes.

PARTNER: I'd like to hand you now what I will mark as Defense Exhibit 46. [Hands the witness a paper.] This is an email from you to the CEO of Company X, correct?

WITNESS: It appears to be from the email addresses here at the top.

PARTNER: Is there anyone else at your company with that email address?

WITNESS: No.

PARTNER: Please read the first paragraph of the email for the record.

WITNESS: Thank you for your invitation to play in your charity softball tournament this weekend. I'm very much looking forward to it. However, your request of three home runs is... quite a stretch... [Witness goes white and sinks in his chair.]

Depositions give litigators a chance to show off their art. The smart litigator, we were told, always has a cup of water (preferably room temperature) on the table beside his client so that, in case the client starts to "go south" and give the wrong answers, his lawyer can casually knock the cup of water into the client's lap to stop the proceeding and give them a chance to confer.

Our instructor was Peter Jacobs, a senior litigation partner. Mostly bald, with thick glasses and a pear-shaped body, Jacobs took his depositions seriously. "The first thing I like to do is to establish mental dominance over the deposition: This is my deposition. I'm calling the shots. I'll tell people where to sit and I'll ask whatever questions I want!" From there we learned how to "clean a witness out." This phrase was probably repeated five hundred times that weekend. It meant leaving witnesses no wiggle room, so they couldn't later change their testimony at trial. Since a witness will have been told by his lawyer to divulge as little information as possible, "cleaning a witness out" involves a ridiculously thorough but necessary method of questioning, which usually goes something like this:

LAWYER: Have you ever been to the White House?

WITNESS: Yes.

LAWYER: How many times?

WITNESS: I don't know.

LAWYER: In the past five years, how many times have you been to the White House?

WITNESS: I don't remember.

LAWYER: Have you been there more than once in the past five years?

WITNESS: Yes.

LAWYER: Have you been there more than ten times in the past five years?

WITNESS: I don't remember.

LAWYER: Have you been there more than five times in the past five years?

WITNESS: Yes.

LAWYER: So, to the best of your recollection, you have been there between five and ten times in the past five years?

WITNESS: Yes.

This pattern is repeated for almost every line of questioning throughout the deposition, which is why depositions are usually long and tedious. Years later, after I took a particularly tedious deposition of a real estate agent in a small town in Northern California, she looked at me sympathetically and said, "I can't believe you do this for a living."

"Tell me about it," I replied.

AFTER DEPOSITION TRAINING, my billable work remained much the same as it had been. All January and February, I pored over financial documents and sifted company records to chart the location of an energy company's coal deposits for the fine print of a financing deal. I spent a week at the company's headquarters reviewing their in-house files on coal seams and excavated piles of coal, slope mines, and shaft mines.

On other cases, I answered discovery requests, which mainly involved repeatedly cutting and pasting the standard objection response: "X objects to this request on the grounds that it is vague, ambiguous, overly broad, and unduly burdensome. X further objects to this request on the basis that it requests documents not reasonably likely to lead to the discovery of admissible evidence. X further objects to this request to the extent that it seeks documents protected by the attorney-client privilege and/or the attorney work product doctrine."

I wrote draft jury instructions for a partner to propose to a judge. This meant little more than finding the right template on the firm's document system and cutting and pasting the names of the parties.

And I did more document reviews.

AFTER SEVERAL EXTENSIONS, the DA's return in opposition to our habeas corpus petition in Mario's case finally arrived on my desk in mid-April 2003. I had been wondering what the DA would say. I thought the evidence of Garcia's incompetence was overwhelming. And considering the absence of credible evidence against Mario, and the fact that there were *only two shooters*, I hoped the DA's office would take a hard look at the case and perhaps see that they had gotten this one wrong. Maybe, even, they wouldn't put up much of a fight. Wasn't it their job to promote justice, and wasn't correcting mistakes of the justice system part of that? I would soon learn just how naïve that assumption was.

The return was massive, about four inches thick. That was not a good sign. I grabbed a pen and started reading. As I read, I began jotting notes in the margin next to points I didn't agree with.

"No," I wrote, we weren't just second-guessing the results of a legitimate trial.

"Wrong," we weren't simply throwing out a "grab bag" of allegations against Garcia, with the benefit of hindsight.

By the third page, I'd written "asshole" for the first time, and by the fifth, I was writing strings of obscenities. According to the DA's office, Anthony Garcia had performed admirably for Mario. They separated each of Garcia's failures that we had alleged, discussed each in isolation, and claimed that each (by itself) did not satisfy the Strickland legal standard for ineffective assistance. The DA's office argued that Garcia's failure to request a separate trial for Mario or to establish that Mario was not a gang member—a key distinction between Mario and his co-defendants—did not amount to ineffective assistance. Neither, they argued, did Garcia's failure to cross-examine witnesses adequately or to call any effective witnesses on Mario's behalf. Any more witnesses for Mario would merely have been "cumulative testimony," they said. And how should Garcia have known to talk to Laurie Nevarez, who had hosted the party at her aunt's house, since, the DA's office argued, Nevarez "couldn't prove that Rocha was innocent."

To me, this was disingenuous and a bold-faced disregard for Garcia's professional duty at the trial stage: to pursue every lead that might raise a reasonable doubt in the minds of jurors. It also ignored the fact that Mario's case depended on eyewitnesses. With no DNA or other physical evidence, it was one witness's word against another's, and there was no way to "prove innocence." Laurie Nevarez was important because, as a witness with no reason to lie on Mario's behalf, her testimony would have undercut Matthew Padilla's identification of Mario as the supposed third driveway shooter, by placing Padilla at a spot where he could not have seen anyone shooting down the driveway. That point was absolutely crucial to Mario's defense. And the law is crystal clear that the *cumulative* effects of a lawyer's errors are to be weighed in determining ineffective assistance of counsel.

With fourteen months of backroom legal experience under my belt, I was naïve about the workings of the criminal justice system and the mind-set of the DA's office. I'd thought their job was to look fairly at the evidence and to prosecute only those they had good reason to believe were guilty. And I'd thought that if they made a mistake, or saw evidence strongly indicating that they had, they would want to correct it. Instead, what we got from them was a knee-jerk defense of the system, full of twisted logic and dubious legal arguments that wouldn't have received a passing grade in law school. I'd thought that stuff was for the dregs of the defense bar, not respected public servants. *Loyalty to the lie,* as Sister Janet called it.

That afternoon, Bob Long called me up to his office to discuss the DA's return. I sputtered, trying to find the right words to express my contempt for it while remaining professional. But this was the first time I had been "poked in the eye" by an opposing lawyer, as litigators like to say, and I couldn't come up with anything better than, "it sucked." "Long-winded and not particularly impressive," Bob said in agreement.

The return was technically submitted on behalf of the People of California, and the names listed on the signature page included the governor, attorney general, and district attorney, surely none of whom had—at this point—heard of the case. The actual author of the brief was a deputy district attorney named Joanne Lach.

"Why don't we give Ms. Lach a call and introduce ourselves?" Bob suggested. That call was pretty unforgettable. Bob said something like:

"Hi, Joanne. This is Bob Long and Ian Graham from Latham & Watkins. We'd like to speak with you briefly about the Rocha case if you have a minute."

Immediately, Lach's voice took on an abrasive tone. She had no interest in talking to us and seemed personally offended that we, as big firm civil litigators, had dared to question the legitimacy of a criminal conviction. She raised her voice and refused to listen to a word Bob said. It was clear that this was going to be a dogfight.

OVER THE NEXT MONTHS, while neck deep in billable work, I spent nights and weekends putting together our response to Lach's return, and preparing for the evidentiary hearing. As the summer of 2003 came to an end and the hearing began to draw closer, Mario's case took over my schedule. The hearing was like a trial, and preparing for a trial—I was learning—is like preparing for a battle. Every detail, tactic, and possibility had to be thought through from every possible angle. Excruciating thought was given to witness lists, presentation of testimony, what exhibits to use, and getting evidence into the record over anticipated objections. I drafted our pretrial brief for Bob Long's review and found and organized the trial exhibits. I recruited Mike White, a former public defender and veteran criminal defense attorney with an impeccable record, who could testify about the standard of competence for defense attorneys at the time of Mario's trial. I worked with our investigator, Aldo

Velasco, to locate potential witnesses, including Laurie Nevarez, and to prepare subpoenas that would require them to appear at trial, if they were not willing to do so voluntarily.

As we prepared, I visited Mario several more times to go over some questions about the night of the shooting to prepare him for the hearing, and at Bob's request, to ask him to grow some hair on his shaved head for his appearance in court. We always met in the same empty room around a small round table. Mario was always polite, but I could tell that he was anxious about the hearing. The last time he had been in a courtroom, things had not gone well. He asked questions about our strategy, who our witnesses were going to be, and what they were going to say. He asked about Laurie Nevarez and why Garcia hadn't called her as a witness at his trial. As we became more familiar with each other, Mario and I also talked about things beyond his case: What his life was like in prison. What he wanted to do if he got out. How much he missed his family. He asked me about my family and my interests. He sent me letters about books he was reading and the writing he was doing. We were becoming friends.

During these visits, I had been struck by Mario's self-control, his ability to remain rational and appear calm in that hard and lonely prison where he did not belong. But in my last visit before the hearing, after I had gone over with him our witness list and what we planned to prove, he seemed visibly shaken. It was the first time he had fully understood how bad his trial defense had been. He took a slow breath and composed himself.

"I want to thank you, Ian. You and Bob, for all you are doing for me. It feels good to know that these deficiencies [in Garcia's representation] are going to be exposed. But at the same time, I think, like, these deficiencies have cost me a lot."

OUR ENTIRE CASE, I knew, would come down to Laurie Nevarez's testimony. Matthew Padilla had been the only semi-credible witness against Mario at his trial. Nevarez had signed a declaration for us two years earlier, under penalty of perjury, placing Padilla in the backyard at the time of the shooting—a position from which he could not possibly have identified anyone shooting down the driveway—and stating that she would have testified to this at trial if Garcia had called her as a witness. If she testified confidently at the evidentiary hearing regarding Padilla's location, then we could satisfy the second prong of the Strickland standard: that but for Garcia's errors and omissions, the outcome of Mario's trial would have been different. "The whole case is Nevarez," Bob said.

A week before the hearing, prosecutor Joanne Lach called to tell me that she and her investigator had visited Laurie Nevarez "to interview" her. I could pick up a tape of the interview at her office, she said, sounding slightly smug. I raced over to the Criminal Courts Building to see what damage, if any, had been done to our star witness. When I listened to the tape, I was aghast. This is from the tape:

LACH: You first hear what you later believe were shots. Do you know where Matthew is, or are you focused on something else?

NEVAREZ: No, Matt was, like I said, walking towards where the two were fighting.

LACH: And it's most important to you to just tell us what you *actually remember*, you actually have a picture in your mind. And not, not a feeling or filler of details.

NEVAREZ: Well, see, I actually thought I saw Matt, but obviously he [pause], well, he says that he wasn't there for the fight, so I mean...

INVESTIGATOR: [interrupts] So what makes you say that you... [Lach interrupts]

LACH: It's what *you* remember... [Investigator interrupts]

INVESTIGATOR: If you don't remember it, then you don't remember it. That's what you have to understand. If you don't remember it, then you don't remember it. That means you don't remember it.

LACH: And you're not being bad if you don't remember. I mean people don't remember some things.

LACH: [a few minutes later] Ok, so, back to this. Is it correct now you don't recall Matthew Padilla being in a particular position when you hear the banging shots that you later determined as shots? You don't *know* where he was at that time.

NEVAREZ: [pause, then meekly, barely audible] Yeah, I don't know where Matt was.

It was more of a brainwashing than an interview. After hearing the tape, we didn't really know what Nevarez would say on the witness stand.

The day before the hearing, I spoke to Mario over the phone. Among other things, he excitedly told me that his family and friends were planning a rally in support of him outside the courthouse on the morning of the hearing, including marches, chanting, and Aztec dancers. "Sounds cool," I said. When I mentioned the planned rally to Bob, he shook his head and said, "We can't have any of that going on. It's not going to help Mario in court and it could be a real problem. You need to go over [to the Rocha house] and you've got to stop that from happening."

After work that evening, I dropped by a pre-hearing gathering of Mario's family at Virginia Rocha's house in Highland Park. Sister Janet was there, along with Virginia Rocha, aunts Bertha and Martha, Mario's father Ralph, brother Danny, cousin David, and others. They were all crowded into the small living room. It was the first time I had met some of the Rocha family, and tensions were high. "Ian has something he would like to say," Sister Janet said, offering me the floor to speak. The room went silent. After explaining a little bit about the procedures for the next day's hearing and what they could expect to see and hear, I cautiously broached the subject of the rally.

"I've been told there is a protest planned for tomorrow..." I began.

"It's a rally, not a protest!" I was quickly corrected by one of Mario's aunts.

"Right, sorry. Rally. That's what I meant to say. We have talked about this at the law firm, and we think it really isn't the best thing for Mario for any distractions to be happening outside the courthouse."

"But this is what Mario wants! This is what we talked to him about," said a cousin.

"I understand. But this is a different kind of hearing. The deck is stacked against us. This judge is going to have to be pretty courageous to overturn Mario's conviction, and we don't want to give him any excuse not to. We don't want him to see the demonstration and say, 'I can't rule for Mario because it will look like I'm caving in to the protest.'"

"You don't understand, Ian," Mario's aunt Bertha began calmly. "I see Mario and he is so tired. He is keeping his head up, but he is so tired." She suddenly became emotional at the image of Mario in prison playing in her mind's eye, and her voice began to rise. "He's been in there for years! For what!? Those people in there, they kill you. They'll kill you if you look at them wrong. We've been through this once! We went to court before and we did nothing, and look at what happened. And now you want us to do nothing again?"

I was speechless. I wasn't going to say another word about the demonstration. But after a moment of tense silence. Mario's brother Danny spoke up. In a slow, deep voice, he said, "If you are telling us it is going to hurt Mario in court, then we won't do it."

"I certainly don't want to *tell* you what to do," I said softly, still a little shaken from Bertha's words. "I understand, or I try to, what you all are going through with this. If you want to demonstrate, I'm not telling you no. But it really is better for Mario if you don't demonstrate." The room fell silent for a few seconds, until Danny nodded his head.

"All right," he said.

I got up to say my good-byes to the family, but suddenly found myself standing in a circle, shoulder to shoulder, and holding hands with the family members and Sister Janet. Everyone bowed their heads as Mario's grandmother said a prayer for the hearing.

—ɯ—

CHAPTER 15

Strike Two

LOS ANGELES, OCTOBER 16–28, 2003

THE HEARING BEGAN on the morning of October 16, 2003, the day after my twenty-ninth birthday. It was the first time I had been in a courtroom as a lawyer. Dressed in my best suit and lugging a litigation bag (a big, rectangular hard-shelled briefcase) filled with exhibits and legal pads, I waded through the security line in the crowded lobby of the downtown Los Angeles Criminal Courts Building and crammed myself into an elevator. I got out at the ninth floor, a high-security area that required passing through a second metal detector and bag scanner, and found my way to Department 105, the Honorable Bob S. Bowers's courtroom.

We had drawn Bowers as our judge and, according to lawyers with experience in front of him, we "could have done worse." He was an experienced Superior Court judge who, according to almost everyone we talked to, was "fair, but not particularly bright."

The hallway outside the courtroom was already packed with Mario's family and supporters. I greeted Mario's mother, cousin David, brother Danny, and aunts Bertha and Martha. Sister Janet was buzzing around in good spirits. "I can't believe this day is finally here!" she said with a big smile. Finally, I spotted Bob Long sitting on a bench outside the courtroom, and I took a seat next to him. "Some showing," he said casually. Mark Geragos, the famed criminal defense lawyer known for having represented Michael Jackson, Gary Condit, and Scott Peterson, among others, stopped by to say hi to Bob and wish him well. A slick-looking criminal defense lawyer in a cheap suit and sunglasses walked up and down the hall yelling, "I am Brandon Starr, which one of you is Hector, my client?"

Bob seemed calm and confident. I was a quivering mass of nerves. Just then, the court clerk opened the door to the courtroom and announced that it was time to begin.

Every seat in the courtroom gallery quickly filled as Mario was led from the holding area and into the courtroom. He held his head up as he shuffled along the floor, tightly shackled at his wrists and ankles. Almost seven years earlier, on his bus ride from Juvenile Hall to the maximum-security prison, he had written of his fear that "this may be my final glimpse" of the "beauty I may never again behold." This was his first time out of prison since then. Thankfully, his mother had been able to get him khaki pants and a dress shirt to wear so he wouldn't be seen in a prison jumpsuit. Mario took his seat next to me at the defense table.

"How are you doing?" I whispered.

"I'm good, man. Just a little nervous."

A few minutes later, Judge Bowers came out of his chambers, took his seat on the bench, and called the proceedings to order.

Bob Long stood up and began his opening statement:

"Today begins the evidentiary hearing on Mr. Rocha's petition for habeas corpus. As the court indicated, this is a hearing on which a determination will be made of whether Mr. Rocha's criminal judgment should be overturned because of ineffective assistance of counsel in his criminal case. We intend to prove in this proceeding that Mr. Rocha's judgment should be overturned, because his trial for murder was so flawed as to be fundamentally unfair to Mr. Rocha and unreliable as an indication of his guilt or innocence. We intend to prove by the preponderance of the evidence, which is our burden, that the flawed trial was the product of the ineffectiveness, ineptitude, errors, and omissions of Mr. Rocha's trial counsel, Anthony Garcia..."

Bob sounded good and was doing well. But Judge Bowers seemed preoccupied with something else. He was reading something, then he began doing paperwork, then whispered something to his clerk. He wasn't even looking at Bob and didn't appear to be listening. *What the hell is Bowers doing?* I thought. Mario nudged me in the shoulder and slid me a note he had written with the two-inch pencil the bailiff had provided him: "He's not paying attention!!!"

When Bob Long finished, Bowers looked up, nodded at Bob, and turned to Lach. Lach's opening statement was curious. She spent most of her time arguing that we, Mario's big-firm, white-shoe attorneys, were improperly trying to relitigate this entire case and didn't understand that the issue was limited to whether or not Mario had received ineffective assistance of counsel at trial.

"Contrary to petitioner's counsel's protestations, the people do believe what's going on here is a retrial of this case with resources and time and money that were not available to Anthony Garcia."

This was surprising, considering that we had never given any indication that we were attempting to broaden the scope of the hearing, and Bob had expressly stated in his opening that we understood the narrow scope of the hearing and that we intended to abide by it. But Lach seemed intent on painting us as naïve, moneyed outsiders. According to Lach, Garcia had put on the "best defense possible" for Mario, and we were simply armchair quarterbacks nit-picking the strategic trial decisions made by Garcia with the benefit of 20/20 hindsight and the "unlimited resources" of Latham & Watkins.

Anthony Garcia took the witness stand. Garcia's appearance alone was a point in our favor. He was short, maybe five-five, even in elevated cowboy boots, and squarely built, with a thick mustache and a braided ponytail that now ran down the length of his back. For the next two and a half days, Bob Long led Garcia step-by-step through his representation of Mario. Garcia admitted to waiting more than five months and only beginning his investigation of Mario's case less than five weeks before the trial was to begin. He offered no explanation for his delay. When his investigation did begin, he hired (with court funds) an investigator named Patrick Sullivan, whom he had told merely to "go out and interview all the witnesses" in the case.

As to the fact that Garcia's files contained only two very

brief written reports of witness interviews by Sullivan, Garcia said he "didn't know" if he relied on written reports or "carried around in [his] brain...the status of the investigation." With time running short before trial, he testified that he had made a strategic decision to narrow the scope of his investigation and focus on alibi witnesses and witnesses who had seen a shooter, thereby excluding Laurie Nevarez, Christina Aragon, and perhaps others who could have undermined Padilla's identification of Mario.

When confronted with the fact that he had spent only eight and one-half hours on the case in the month leading up to trial, Garcia replied that he had worked additional time on the case but must not have recorded it. He admitted that he had never interviewed the occupants of the home where the party and shooting took place and had never asked his investigator to do so. He had no recollection of ever trying to find out who had organized the party. He claimed that his trial strategy was to point the finger at the two other defendants, but he could not cite a single example in the trial in which he did so.

Bob hammered home example after example of how Garcia had failed to emphasize crucially important exonerating evidence for Mario during the trial: evidence that there were only two shooters (Garcia told the trial judge and jury that he "wasn't even going to address that"); evidence that Mario's two co-defendants were known, documented Highland Park gang members, and that Mario was not; the shaky identifications of Mario as the third driveway shooter by Bryan Villalobos and Lauro Mendoza, whom Garcia did not effectively cross-examine. (Mendoza was on record in the preliminary hearing before the trial as having said he "wasn't sure" of his identification, and Villalobos had given our investigator a sworn statement saying he was only 50 percent sure of his identification of Mario.)

Finally, Bob asked Garcia about his cross-examination of Matthew Padilla regarding his identification of Mario as the left-handed driveway shooter:

LONG: Did you recognize that in this account [Padilla's statement to police identifying Mario], according to the detective, Mr. Padilla was saying that the person he saw, who he identified as Mr. Rocha, had kneeled down on his right knee and then placed the gun in his left hand and fired six to seven shots?

GARCIA: No, I don't. I don't remember that.

LONG: Okay, let me ask you to turn your attention to the second page, about the third line down, beginning with the sentence "The guy then kneeled down on his right knee and then placed the gun in his left hand and fired about six to seven shots."

GARCIA: I am looking at that, yes, sir.

LONG: Did you ever ask Mario whether he was right-handed or left-handed?

GARCIA: [long pause] I don't remember.

"You can't tell from the transcript," Long would later say about his left-handed/right-handed question to Garcia, "but if you were in the courtroom at the time, you could see Garcia just look up at me for a long second with a look on his face that said, 'Oh my.'"

Bob kept an even tone, adding emphasis only when necessary to make a point clear. He let the evidence and Garcia's own admissions do the talking. Even so, it was the most thorough, nonviolent pummeling of a human being I had ever seen.

On cross-examination, Lach tried to rehabilitate Garcia by offering him a chance to explain his decisions as strategic and made under the stress of a trial. But by the time Garcia wearily limped off the stand, I figured we had won round one.

Virginia Rocha took the stand next to testify briefly that Mario is right-handed.

Bob Long had added to our defense team a junior partner named Marcus McDaniel, to handle the questioning of Laurie Nevarez and of our investigator, Aldo Velasco. "Nothing against the job you are doing," Bob had told me, "but I have my hands full with Garcia. Marcus is excellent in a courtroom, and perhaps a life-and-death trial isn't the best time for you to take your first witness." I couldn't have agreed more. Marcus, an African American in his early forties, was an experienced and unflappable employment litigator.

Marcus called to the stand Aldo Velasco, who testified that he had found Laurie Nevarez simply by going to the crime scene and speaking to the owners of the house. Almost immediately, Lach objected to Velasco's entire testimony as irrelevant. "Whatever might have occurred two, three, four years later is not relevant to the issue of what this attorney did back in 1997 and whether that was reasonable or not."

Marcus countered that it was entirely relevant that Velasco, even years later, was able to locate Nevarez simply by visiting the crime scene and that Nevarez had signed a declaration stating not only that she would have talked to defense counsel had they contacted her in 1997, but also that she would have testified at trial that Padilla was in the backyard at the time of the shooting, where he could not have seen who fired shots down the driveway.

Judge Bowers mumbled for a moment and then sustained the objection, refusing to let Velasco testify.

Then Laurie Nevarez took the stand. It was clear that she was frightened by the courtroom and that she didn't want to be there. She spoke almost in a whisper and had to be admonished by Judge Bowers to speak up. Marcus led her through her involvement in organizing the party and her connection to Matthew Padilla, whom she described as having been a friend at the time of the party. She said she did not know Mario Rocha and had no reason to lie on his behalf. Using an overhead projection, Marcus asked Nevarez to show and explain the place, in front of the tarp that separated the driveway from the backyard, where Padilla stood during most of the party, the place where the fight broke out, and the place where she, Nevarez, was standing when the first shots were fired.

These questions and answers set up the testimony on which Mario's future depended. You could feel the tension at our defense table as Marcus McDaniel carefully asked Laurie Nevarez questions intended to show whether Matthew Padilla's identification of Mario as the driveway shooter should have been believed or could have been discredited by Nevarez if Anthony Garcia had called her to testify:

McDANIEL: Did there come a point that you saw Mr. Padilla at the time that you and Ms. Aragon were observing the argument?

NEVAREZ: Yes.

McDANIEL: And where did you see Mr. Padilla located?

NEVAREZ: I believe walking towards us.

McDANIEL: Toward you in the backyard?

NEVAREZ: Yes.

McDANIEL: And this was at the time of the argument?

NEVAREZ: Yes.

McDANIEL: Did you at some point see the argument turn into a fight?

NEVAREZ: Yes. I believe it was during the fight that Christina hollered for Matthew.

McDANIEL: Did you see Mr. Padilla during the fight?

NEVAREZ: I believe just coming towards us.

McDANIEL: And Mr. Padilla was on the backside of the tarp, is that correct?

NEVAREZ: Yes.

McDANIEL: Did there come a point when you heard shots ring out?

NEVAREZ: Yes.

McDANIEL: How much time would you estimate took place between the time you saw Mr. Padilla walk toward the argument and when the shots rang out?

NEVAREZ: Everything happened really fast...I think it's when he was walking towards us already that's when the shots started happening right away.

McDANIEL: So your recollection is that as soon as you saw Mr. Padilla walking towards you, toward the argument in the backyard, you heard the shots?

NEVAREZ: Yes.

McDANIEL: You were able to recognize Mr. Padilla?

NEVAREZ: Yes.

McDANIEL: And he's still in the backyard?

NEVAREZ: Yes.

McDANIEL: Were you ever contacted by an attorney or investigator about what you had seen at the party prior to the 1997 trial relating to the shootings at the party?

NEVAREZ: No.

McDANIEL: If you had been contacted by an attorney or investigator and asked what you had seen at the party, would you have told them what you saw?

NEVAREZ: Yes.

McDANIEL: Would you have appeared in court and testified about what you saw?

NEVAREZ: Yes.

McDANIEL: Let me ask you this, Ms. Nevarez. Do you recall a time when you were interviewed by Ms. Lach and an investigator from the District Attorney's Office?

NEVAREZ: Yes.

McDANIEL: Do you recall being asked during that interview when it was that you saw Mr. Padilla move into the backyard?

NEVAREZ: Yes. I told them that I saw him, but I wasn't sure if it was from the side of me or where, but I did see Matthew coming into the backyard.

McDANIEL: Prior to the fight?

NEVAREZ: Yes.

McDANIEL: Do you recall how many times you were asked when you saw Padilla coming into the backyard before the shots rang out?

NEVAREZ: Yes. A lot. They kept asking me and asking me.

McDANIEL: And you kept giving the same response?

NEVAREZ: Yes.

McDANIEL: Did you feel like you were being pressured in that interview?

NEVAREZ: Yes.

McDANIEL: And were you uncomfortable?

NEVAREZ: Yes. I felt like I was on trial or I did something wrong. I was trying to answer as best I could, but things I would say and they would say, "Are you sure? Are you sure? It wasn't this way? It wasn't that way?"

Joanne Lach's cross-examination of Nevarez lasted an entire afternoon. Lach had found small inconsistencies between the statement Nevarez had given investigator Aldo Velasco in 1999 and her testimony here in court, and tried to use them to discredit her. Nevarez wasn't sure if she was standing directly in the spot she had identified in her statement or three feet to the left. She wasn't sure if, when he entered the backyard, Padilla had walked directly toward her or slightly off to the side.

"You're worried that you signed a declaration in 1999, under the penalty of perjury, that has mistakes in it, aren't you!?" Lach thundered at her.

Laurie Nevarez had heard enough. For the first time, she sat upright in her chair and leaned into the microphone.

"No, I'm just here to say what I know."

I pumped my fist under the table. We had won right there, I thought.

The next morning, Christina Aragon, Matthew Padilla's girlfriend at the time of the shooting, took the stand. Although she claimed not to remember anything and was a reluctant witness, she admitted that she had signed a declaration for Aldo Velasco corroborating Nevarez's account that Padilla was in the backyard when the shots were fired, and stating that she would have testified as much if she had been called at trial.

Our last witness was Mike White, our expert in criminal defense practice. White's credentials included thirty years of criminal trial practice, six as a public defender, most of it in Los Angeles County courtrooms. He had handled more than one hundred jury trials, forty of them murder cases, fifteen of which were gang-related. He was a lecturer for the California Bar Association on cases involving multiple defendants. Prior to testifying, he had reviewed the transcripts of Mario's original trial and Anthony Garcia's entire file. Questioned by Bob Long, White testified at length and described in detail how Garcia's representation of Mario had, under the prevailing professional standards as they existed in 1997, fallen woefully short of what a defense lawyer should reasonably have done in this case. White was an excellent witness, getting his points across clearly and speaking in a compelling manner. Lach went at him hard in cross-examination, trying to make him out to be an expert witness for hire who was there simply to second-guess Garcia's tactics, but White held firm.

Overall, we felt the hearing had gone very well for us. Bob, Marcus, and I met with Mario briefly in the holding tank outside the courtroom. He was in high spirits. "I don't want to get my hopes up too much," he said, "but I think the judge will see the truth this time." "I hope so. Stay strong," Bob told him. In the hallway outside the courtroom, Bob addressed Mario's family and friends and Sister Janet: "I think it went well, but this is a difficult process. We'll just have to see what happens." But on the elevator ride down, alone with Marcus and me, he said what we were all thinking: "I think we've got a very good shot at this judge ordering a new trial for Mario."

—⁂—

CHAPTER 16

As Good As It Gets

Some certain dregs of conscience are yet within me.

—Shakespeare, *Richard III*

LATHAM & WATKINS, DECEMBER 2003–2004

THE LATHAM & WATKINS Christmas party wasn't exactly the elegant evening affair one might expect from one of the largest, most profitable law firms in the world. It was held from two to four on a Wednesday afternoon in a reception room at the California Club, LA's oldest private social club, a block from the office. Apart from a few decorations scattered about the paneled room, there was little evidence of a festive spirit. Lawyers milled around talking mostly about work. A few partners prowled the room looking for associates who owed them work. Associates bobbed and weaved to avoid them. A two-drink maximum was enforced, with drink tickets handed out upon arrival.

I spotted Trevor Wilson sitting at a small empty table against the wall and went over to join him. Since our first document review assignment in San Diego, Trevor had been stuck working healthcare cases, reviewing documents, and coming up with explanations of why hospital after hospital had "mistakenly," instead of fraudulently, overbilled Medicare. He had unintentionally put himself in a good position with the Healthcare Litigation Group, where he was well regarded by the partners and associates, but he was struggling with the work he was doing and the path on which his career seemed headed. I wasn't altogether surprised. From a small town outside of Santa Barbara, Trevor had joined Latham out of UCLA Law School for the same reasons I had: he had gotten caught up in the prestige, the money, and the fun of the summer associate experience, and for a time, he had enjoyed the new car and fancy clothes his Latham paycheck made possible. But the real Trevor was at heart an earnest, salt-of-the-earth small-town rancher.

"This job has no soul," he said as we sat there nursing the second of our two allotted drinks. "I don't do anything. I don't make anything. I clean up other people's messes and write memos about it," he said. "I don't admire any of the people I work for or want to be like them in any way." His problem, if you can call it that, he knew, would most likely be fatal to his career at a big firm like this one: he needed to find meaning in his work. A few months later, Trevor left Latham to become an attorney for the federal government, investigating and pursuing fraudulent HMO billing practices.

Until recently, I hadn't thought I carried that burden. When I joined Latham I'd believed it fit exactly who I was: a capitalist at heart, unapologetic about liking material things. I didn't need to find meaning in anything as long as the money was right.

Or so I thought. Two years at Latham had produced some unexpected changes in me. After I had watched guards bring Mario in shackles to our meetings in the prison cafeteria, after I had sat facing him as we talked about his life in prison and his hopes for a life after it—knowing that he and his family and Sister Janet were depending on me and the Latham team for his only chance at freedom—thoughts about what I was doing and why came involuntarily on those long drives back to Los Angeles. I tried to push them away, but they kept coming back, not yet fully formed or understood, but increasingly present. I was developing a goddamned conscience.

I BECAME CONCERNED when the new year arrived without a decision from Judge Bowers. I'd figured that if Bowers intended to rule in our favor, he would do it quickly in order to start the process of setting things right. When the decision didn't come, I told myself that maybe the judge was just taking his time with his ruling in order to get it right and protect himself in case the state wanted to appeal. I said this to Mario over the phone and to Sister Janet when she called at least once a week, trying to sound reassuring. But I was getting nervous.

With the beginning of 2004, I became a third-year associate. My two-year purgatory as a lowly unassigned associate had ended, and I joined the Litigation Department. On the upside, this meant an end to the Friday afternoon "emergency" emails from The Book, which assigned weekend document reviews and due diligence work to any associate who appeared to have the time. And it meant I was no longer under Adam Greene's thumb.

But it also meant that I could no longer rely on the The Book for work. I would have to network with the litigation partners and senior associates to get staffed on their cases, and I would have to perform well enough for them to keep me in mind for future cases. Over the next few years, it would be up to me to get experience in the full range of litigation skills—discovery, depositions, motion writing, court appearances—as I laid the foundation for my career as a litigator.

Most of the third-years who were joining the Litigation Department were hitting the ground running. They were already working on active cases for several partners, and they had already cultivated a pipeline of work that would keep them going for the foreseeable future. I was hitting the ground with a thud. My only real litigation experience so far, other than a few document reviews on which I was one anonymous member of a large team, was Mario's case. Steve Newman had left the firm, and Bob Long, to my surprise, had announced that he was retiring from the firm at the end of 2004. By my count, Marcus McDaniel and John Oliver were the only two litigation partners who knew I existed. Oliver was busy with a trial in San Diego, and McDaniel, an employment litigator, had just settled a few cases and didn't have any work available for me.

Until now I had done most of my billable work for mid-level and senior associates. So over the next few days, I emailed every Litigation Department associate I knew or was even vaguely familiar with, announcing that I had capacity to take on new work; but none of them had anything for me. I came to realize that some of them viewed me differently now that I was a third-year in their department. I was now a rival for billable hours and the attention of partners they had been cultivating, not a rookie, fair game for anonymous backroom work. I began walking the halls, introducing myself to a few partners in the department and asking if they had anything for me. Nothing. I began emailing other partners, asking for work. No response. As the days of no work turned into weeks, I began to panic. Turning in time sheets that read "0.6 hours—professional reading," which meant I had read the *Daily Journal*, a law-related newspaper, was not the way to start out in the Litigation Department. For three weeks I was completely idle. I began sending out more emails asking for work and saving them as evidence, in case anyone wanted to know what the hell I had been doing all day.

During this time, a headhunter (or legal recruiter) called to ask if I would be interested in hearing about some great firms that were looking to hire third-year associates. Headhunters call law firm associates frequently, but I had always dismissed them with a curt "not interested, thank you." Moving to another firm had never made sense to me. No matter what firms say, the work at all big firms is generally the same. If I moved, I would only be starting all over again with a bunch of strangers. And I would be leaving Mario in the lurch. Steve Newman had already left. Bob Long would be retiring soon. Marcus McDaniel, who had stepped in and performed remarkably at the evidentiary hearing, wasn't totally invested in the case yet. I was the only continuity. I felt terrible for even thinking about leaving.

Still, I feared my days might be numbered anyway. At any moment, I expected the head of the Litigation Department to storm into my office and demand to know exactly what I had been doing for the past month. But there was no work for me at Latham, or for whatever reason, nobody seemed to want to work with me. Reluctantly, I agreed to meet with the headhunters.

They suggested we meet at an out-of-the way place where no one from Latham would see us talking. When I arrived at the Santa Monica café we had selected, the whole thing felt kind of dirty. The two headhunters—a dumpy, disheveled man somewhere between the ages of thirty and fifty, and a large, overeager middle-aged woman—insisted on talking in whispers, furtively glancing around as if someone in the café might overhear us and report back to Latham. They said they had set up three interviews for me with international "first-tier" firms similar to Latham. They were excited, the woman almost too much so, going on and on about how wonderful and "collegial" these firms were. They told me to "smile" in the interviews and to talk about my "passion for law practice."

It was a very different hiring process from the one I had experienced coming out of law school. I had been riding high then, or thought I was, and had wanted the job. Now, having been at a firm for over two years, I knew I didn't love the work, but I needed the job. I had a mortgage and a fancy car to pay for. Recognizing this, I sucked it up, put on a happy face, and hit the interview circuit again.

I had offers from all three firms where I interviewed. The headhunters were panting and almost delirious. They started pushing me toward one of the firms. I assumed they stood to earn the biggest commission if I accepted that one. I ignored much of what they said. To me, the other big LA firms were all pretty much the same. They looked the same, had the same specialized departments, competed for the same clients, and paid about the same. One firm, however, which happened to be the one the headhunters favored, had the advantage of having its offices in Santa Monica. I could get from my house to the office in five minutes, without fighting LA freeway traffic.

I decided to give Latham another week, to see if anything changed. Each day I sent out more emails asking for work. No responses. I ate lunch in the attorney dining room (usually a significant hazard for overloaded associates) and stared eagerly at anyone in the Litigation Department. Nothing. Finally, depressed about the whole situation, I accepted the Santa Monica firm's offer.

I had thought about calling Mario to talk to him about it before accepting, but I couldn't bring myself to do it.

A few hours after accepting the offer, I gave my two weeks' notice to Latham's human resources manager and then sent an email to Bob Long telling him that I was leaving the firm and had given Latham my notice. I told him how much I had enjoyed working with him on Mario's case.

I wasn't expecting a response, and if I did get one, I expected it to be something along the lines of "don't let the door hit you in the ass on the way out." But within minutes, Bob responded: "Ian, this is surprising news, and I certainly hope this isn't an undoable decision. I'd like to talk to you as soon as possible about this and hope we can keep you here at Latham. How about lunch tomorrow?"

At Café Pinot, one of downtown LA's best restaurants, Bob

began recruiting me all over again. My work on Mario's case, he said, had been commendable and had shown him I had what it took to succeed at Latham. "What can we do to keep you here?" he asked. I explained that I hadn't wanted to leave, but that I had not been able to find any work. "I've been sitting on my hands for almost a month," I said.

"That's the firm's fault, not yours," he said. "This place has grown so rapidly and to such a staggering size that sometimes associates can slip through the cracks."

Although Bob was in the process of retiring and didn't personally have any work for me, he could see to it that I was given plenty of interesting work that would pave the way for my future at the firm.

"I would urge you not to make any final decision right now," he said. "If you are open to the possibility of staying, which I truly hope you are, think about it for a few days and let me see what I can do." I agreed to give it some thought.

Minutes after I got back to my office, Teddy McMillan, a senior partner in the Litigation Department, stopped by to introduce himself.

"I've been following the Rocha case for a while," he said, "and I've heard some very good things about your work. You've managed to impress some serious people here, and I'd like to do what I can to keep you here. What can we do?"

I told him about my lack of work, that I had already accepted an offer at another firm, and that I wasn't sure I could back out of it.

"Of course you can. People do that stuff all the time," Teddy said. "I've got some pull around this place and can see to it that we get you up and running. Think about it, and please call or swing by anytime if you want to talk about this, or anything."

Later that afternoon, Marc Peterson, a tax partner who had just taken over for Elaine Sherman as the LA office managing partner, stopped by my office. He was remarkably soft-spoken and genuine.

"I just wanted to talk to you about this situation and let you know that we would truly like to keep you here. I think you have a bright future here if you give us the chance to fix this. We certainly don't do this for everybody, and that speaks to how well you are regarded here."

With Bob Long's support, by working on a pro bono case, and without intending to, I had put myself on the fast track. I agreed to stay.

My first case arrived by email the following day.

"I hear you're looking to get some 'interesting work,'" wrote David Lowen a fast-rising junior partner. "Take a look at the attachment and give me a buzz."

As I clicked on the email attachment, my secretary, Debbie, walked in to deliver some mail. Just as she neared the corner of my desk, with a perfect view of my computer monitor, the rear view of a young woman, completely naked, bent over at the waist with her hands grasping her ankles and her face looking back at the camera from between her legs, filled my screen.

"Oh God!" I blurted. "Sorry, it's not what it looks like."

"It never is," said Debbie as she walked out, closing the door behind her.

I called Lowen, wondering if this was some kind of joke. He chuckled and explained that, no, this was a real case, or about to be. The picture was part of a German pornographic magazine article, and the woman in the picture was claiming she had never consented to have her *face* shown in the magazine. She was threatening to sue our client, a large international magazine publisher. My job was to research the law and write a stern letter to the woman's attorney explaining that she had no legal claim against the publisher and that if they proceeded with a lawsuit, not only would she lose, but we would come after her for reimbursement for our legal fees.

"She's staring right into the camera, for God's sake," said Lowen.

Then Tom Coleman, a gray-haired, chain-smoking senior partner, called me about a case for a developer who was partnering with an Indian tribe to build a casino on a reservation near Sacramento. Our client had bought land next to the reservation to use for parking and other casino facilities, but after an article announcing the casino development appeared in the local newspaper, the sellers were now suing to break the deal, claiming they would not have sold the land had they known of its intended use. The developer was countersuing to force the deal through. The case was headed for trial, and a string of depositions needed to be taken quickly.

After getting up to speed on all the facts and contracts in play, I drafted deposition outlines and scripts for Coleman and attended five depositions he took in Sacramento, handing him exhibits as he fired questions at the witnesses. When Coleman was unavailable, I took my first deposition of the landowners and, to my surprise, managed to back the witness into a corner to the point where he refused to answer any questions that might hurt the plaintiff's case. The video of my deposition ended up being played in full at the trial, after which our client's general counsel whispered to me, "Great fucking job." I drafted the pre- and post-trial briefs and handled the questioning of a witness at the trial.

Another senior partner sent me a case file with instructions to "handle this and make it go away." Like the German porno case, this one was also grimly comical. A wealthy middle-aged man from Texas had come to Los Angles by himself on Christmas Day, checked into a luxury hotel in Santa Monica, and taken a taxi to a casino in the tough neighborhood of Inglewood. Surveillance tapes from the casino showed him gambling and drinking for several hours, then leaving with a large tattooed and menacing-looking man, who later beat him severely with an iron in his hotel room. The attacker had been arrested and convicted, but the victim, now facially disfigured, was suing the casino, the casino operator, and the casino's parent company for negligence in allowing him to get beaten up in his hotel room fifteen miles from the casino by a man with whom he'd voluntarily left the casino. Latham represented the casino owner. The plaintiff's attorney, a solo practitioner in Manhattan Beach, was apparently hoping for a settlement.

As in the German porno case, I wrote a stern letter to the plaintiff's attorney, explaining that he had no legal basis to sue my client and warning him that if he did, we would come after him for legal fees once the case was dismissed. When he ignored me, I took the plaintiff's deposition, which had to be stopped periodically when the plaintiff's reconstructed jaw locked. I drafted a motion for summary judgment and ultimately got the case dismissed.

I also worked on a case for Marcus McDaniel involving a claim of wrongful termination filed by a doctor against a local hospital, alleging, among other things, discrimination based on national origin. "How does an American hospital discriminate against an American doctor on the basis of national origin?" I asked. "Exactly," replied Marcus. This got me my first courtroom argument experience. I spent weeks drafting a demurrer motion (also called the "so what" motion), arguing that even if his claims were true, which they weren't, there was no violation of the law, and I argued it in court. I prepared obsessively for the oral argument, trying to anticipate the judge's questions and hoping I wouldn't make a fool of myself. When the case was called, I introduced myself: "Ian Graham of Latham & Watkins on behalf of the defendant," and then didn't say another word. The judge spent the next ten minutes grilling the plaintiff's lawyer about the holes in his case, and then said to me:

"Mr. Graham, do you have anything to add?"

"No, Your Honor. I think you covered it well," I responded.

He granted the motion. Case closed.

This was as good as it gets for a third-year associate. I was receiving plum assignments, working with partners, and earning favorable reviews. By the firm's standards, I was doing very well, especially considering that one-third of my first-year class had already left the firm.

But my life outside the firm was disappearing. The long days and constant pressure to bill hours and produce flawless work, no matter how tight the deadlines or conflicting the demands, were taking a toll. I saw less and less of friends, who were all doing well and seeming to enjoy more balanced lives. I skipped family vacations and holidays. I dated, but it was almost impossible to maintain a relationship when my nights and weekends were spent at the office. The constant adversarial process—facing someone equally prepared and motivated whose mission was to rip apart everything I did—was wearing.

Some people thrive on this kind of work. I didn't. At night I would lie awake for hours, panicked that I had missed something in a brief or had incorrectly numbered exhibits—all to fix the problems of some corporation.

And those nagging, involuntary thoughts that had begun on the long drives from Calipatria to LA wouldn't go away. Mario and his case had seeped into my sense of what I was doing, and had brought changes. In spite of myself, I couldn't help caring about the social value, or lack of it, of what I did. And that—even more than worry over mistakes in briefs or exhibits—also kept me awake at night.

Teddy McMillan called frequently to check up on me. "Are we getting you enough work?" he asked jokingly. Knowing I had played baseball in college, he asked me to help him represent a Major League Baseball team in a dispute with their insurance company over a policy covering payments owed to the team for an injured player. After I got up to speed on the case, McMillan took me with him to the stadium to meet with the owner, general manager, and general counsel, to discuss strategies and anticipated outcomes. A few months later, he sent me alone to meet with the injured player and represent him during his deposition.

It doesn't get any better than that for a junior lawyer in a big firm: working with one of the top partners and getting client contact with a Major League Baseball team and player. But—tellingly—for me, it only confirmed that big-firm practice and I were a bad fit.

I had played baseball in high school with the team's general manager, and I had played with one of their players in college. We had mutual friends who were baseball players, baseball executives, and sports agents. They were all about my age, were not worn down by their jobs, and were doing something they were passionate about. Ironically, McMillan's giving me this coveted assignment left me more dissatisfied than ever about grinding away at a law firm job I wasn't suited for. Even working with a Major League Baseball team, I was still researching the fine print of insurance contracts and preparing depositions in a fight between corporations over money.

It was great work for someone who really wanted to make it in a big firm. But it helped me realize that I didn't. Still, I had invested years at Latham, and the fear of leaving a steady, substantial paycheck kept me going.

—~—

CHAPTER 17

A Lengthy Process

LOS ANGELES, 2004

In late August 2004, ten months after we had concluded the evidentiary hearing in Mario's case, Judge Bowers's ruling arrived: DENIED.

Bowers wrote, "Now that an evidentiary hearing was held, it is clear that no witnesses existed who could prove Petitioner's innocence as he claimed. The testimony presented failed to raise credible evidence of Petitioner's innocence by a preponderance of the evidence. [Petitioner] has failed to show that his attorney did not act promptly in conducting an investigation of this case [and] failed to identity *any* evidence that his attorney would have obtained if the investigation had been conducted swifter."

This was devastating. Evidentiary hearings are seldom granted. We had presented our best case, which we thought was overwhelming, and had lost. And under the law, Bowers's findings and ruling would be given considerable weight in any further proceedings. To succeed in an appeal, we would not only, again have to prove that Garcia had rendered ineffective assistance of counsel, but also, now, convince a court that an experienced Superior Court judge who had heard all of our evidence and witnesses was dead wrong.

For all practical purposes, Mario's case now looked unwinnable.

Bob Long, Marcus McDaniel, and I gathered in Bob's office to deliver the news to Mario in a speakerphone call.

"Good morning, attorneys!" Mario greeted us with excitement.

"Good morning to you, Mario," Bob began somberly. "I wish we were calling with better news, but the court has denied our petition."

Mario had already heard about the denial from his family, and as Bob started to speak, Mario interrupted. "It's okay. I'm already handling it," he said.

Bob shook his head, as if to say, "How on earth can you handle this?"

"Well, we're not handling it so well here, you might say. In all respects, we are disappointed with the judge's ruling."

"What's the next step?" Mario asked. And after a pause, he added, "Is there a next step?"

"Well, the next step is to go back to the Court of Appeal to appeal this decision," Bob said, sounding grim. "And then the California Supreme Court after that, and then the federal system after that. But I think it's safe to say that this is going to be a lengthy process."

"Lengthy processes are what I'm used to," Mario said, forcing a laugh. "Time is something I've got plenty of."

Bob shook his head again at Mario's resilience. "We are going to stay with this to the..." Bob caught himself and paused for a second to find the right words, "...until we get the right result."

After Bob hung up the phone, he turned to Marcus and me and said, "How does he do it? How does he manage to keep his head up when he keeps getting the raw end of it at every turn?"

Then he looked at me and said, "You've got to go point by point through this judge's ruling and knock it down. Because he's wrong. He's just wrong."

Drafting a new habeas petition to the Court of Appeal, picking apart the findings of a Superior Court judge, would require long hours of research and writing with virtually no chance of success. And I didn't have a lot of time to spare. In addition to working on my baseball case with Teddy McMillan, and the casino case with Tom Coleman, I had recently gotten a call from Bert Adler, one of Latham's superstar litigation partners and biggest rainmakers. He and Teddy McMillan were good friends, and Teddy had given him a favorable scouting report on me. "I've got a case for you," Adler said. You didn't say no to Bert Adler. At Latham, it was considered a big opportunity to work for him. He had the clout to make partners of associates.

But Adler had made millions for himself and the firm by coldly and effectively defending toxic waste dumpers and gun manufacturers, among others such clients. It was rumored around Latham that he kept on a shelf in his office a drop of chromium 6, the toxic chemical alleged to have caused cancer clusters in one of his toxic tort cases.

Adler wanted me to help defend a large company accused of dumping toxic chemicals into the groundwater in Nevada, causing cancer clusters and leukemia in a nearby town. My assignment was to fight the plaintiffs' request for an expedited trial by writing a brief arguing that—although many of the plaintiffs under the age of thirteen and over the age of seventy were dying of cancer—they couldn't prove they were going to die within a year, and therefore they were not sick enough to warrant speeding up the trial date. It felt like a dirty assignment on behalf of an allegedly dirty client. And yet, I couldn't help but like Adler as a person. He was a genial guy, had a sharp wit, and as a lawyer he was brilliant. He thought, talked, and worked at hyper speed, and I found myself wanting to impress him by doing a good job.

Over the next month, I spent my days drafting the motion for Adler's toxic groundwater case. I reviewed the plaintiffs' medical records and their deposition testimony, and twisted their words to take advantage of any ambiguity or misstatement in their medical diagnoses. Bert loved my draft of the motion. He barely changed a word, and I heard he argued my brief flawlessly in court. The judge ruled for us, denying those plaintiffs their expedited day in court.

And while I worked on Bert Adler's toxic tort case, I spent my nights, evenings, and weekends working on Mario's appeal of Judge Bowers's ruling—showing how the DA's office and the prosecutor at Mario's trial had twisted testimony and sown confusion in the minds of jurors.

The contrast between my billable work by day and my unbillable work for Mario at night was hard to take. Before Mario's case, I might not have thought twice about working on Bert Adler's case. Lawyers are hired to argue for their clients,

I believed. They represent clients, not causes. It was up to the voters and the legislature to change the laws if they didn't like them.

But I didn't really believe that anymore. How different was what I had done for Bert Adler, and others, from what the prosecutors had done in Mario's case? Was I willing to excuse Mario's prosecutors for "just doing their job?" Maybe my job in a private law firm was different from that of a public servant—in my billable work, I was indeed paid to represent clients, not causes—but was that the end of my personal responsibility? Never mind the tedium of much of law practice; if my conscience conflicted too much with my job description a lot of the time, then maybe I needed to rethink my job.

FOR MONTHS I WORKED obsessively on the new habeas petition. I spent weeks poring over the transcripts of the evidentiary hearing, pulling together pieces of testimony to contradict Bowers's findings. I turned the living room of my new home into a war room, with pleadings, transcripts, and case files scattered everywhere. As Bob had instructed, I went point by point through Bowers's flawed ruling, knocking down his findings one by one.

The one ray of hope for Mario was that Bowers's ruling was so poorly written and reasoned that it opened the door very slightly for an appeal. Bowers ruled that we had failed to prove Mario was innocent—an issue that was not before the court and that he had previously admonished us was not relevant to the hearing. In response to Joanne Lach's argument in her opening statement that we were improperly trying to relitigate the entire case and offer evidence of Mario's actual innocence (instead of focusing on Garcia's ineffective assistance of counsel), Bowers had agreed with Lach. As he warned us, "[I]t is not this court's intention to relitigate this trial. We have a very specific mandate from the Court of Appeal, and I intend to abide by that." We had abided and been punished for it. In his ruling, Bowers wrote, "It is clear no witness exists who could have proven Petitioner's innocence as he claimed. The testimony failed to raise credible evidence of Petitioner's innocence by a preponderance of the evidence."

Bowers found that Laurie Nevarez was not a credible witness, despite the fact that she never wavered in her testimony that Padilla was in a place where he could not have seen Mario firing down the driveway, as he had claimed.

Bowers even found a witness "not credible" who *had not even testified.* The ruling made it look sadly as though Judge Bowers had not taken the hearing seriously and had not paid attention.

Looking for any advantage I could find, I remembered the witness statement in the police files implicating the third Highland Park gang member, Joker, who had crashed the party along with Pee Wee and Cartoon. I cited and described the statement in a footnote of our petition to the Court of Appeal, emphasizing that I had gotten the information from the police files.

NEAR THE END of 2004, while I was still working on our appeal of Judge Bowers's ruling, I received my first negative review from the firm. The comments from the partners I had worked with were all very positive. I got great reviews from Bob Long, Bert

Adler, and Teddy McMillan. But the firm's formal message to me addressed only one thing: "Your billable hours are below pace for the class of 2001. Failure to maintain billable hours pace could negatively affect your future at the firm."

—∾—

CHAPTER 18

What's This?

LOS ANGELES AND CALIPATRIA, 2005

We filed our appeal of Judge Bowers's ruling in January 2005. Remarkably, three months later, the Court of Appeal came through for Mario, again ordering the DA's office to show cause why our habeas corpus petition challenging Mario's conviction should not be granted.

And this time the Court of Appeal ordered a one-hour oral argument before a three-justice panel of the Court of Appeal on the basis of the evidence presented at Judge Bowers's hearing.

Mario would have another shot, this time with some hope that the pendulum was swinging his way. But the greatest personal trial for Mario—and for me—was about to begin.

The day after we received the favorable Court of Appeal ruling, I called the prison to arrange a phone call with Mario to tell him the good news. Instead of the usual straightforward procedure, I was bounced around and finally passed to the prison information officer. He told me Mario was in the infirmary.

"Is he okay?" I asked.

"I can't give out that information," he said coldly.

"Is he sick? Can you at least tell me the nature of the problem?"

The information officer was silent for a few seconds and then said slowly, "It was a stabbing. He was stabbed."

I was speechless. Immediately, I thought about the police report mentioning Joker that I had inserted in our last habeas petition. The attack on Mario might be my fault.

Unable to get any other information from the prison, I called Mario's cousin, David. David was my primary contact with the Rocha family. He and Mario had grown up together and were like brothers. A city employee and pee wee football coach, David was solidly built and had tattoos covering his shoulder and upper arm, but had an easygoing manner and a friendly smile.

"David?"

"Ian, hey, what's up? How you doing?" he asked cheerfully.

"I'm good, but, um, I'm afraid I've got some bad news. I just talked to someone at Calipatria who told me Mario was stabbed and is in the infirmary."

David's tone changed instantly. "What happened? Tell me what happened?"

"I don't know at this point, I'm afraid. They won't tell me anything other than he is in the infirmary. The information officer I spoke to said they can only give medical information to family members, so you or someone from the family should call."

"Okay," David said quickly. "I'll call you back."

The next morning, David dropped by my office. We walked quickly from the reception area to my office and shut the door.

"A couple of guys jumped him," David said.

"How bad is he hurt?" I asked.

"He's okay. Nothing too serious. One of the blades went through his forearm."

"Holy Christ," I gasped, visualizing the attack for a moment. "Is this about what I think it's about? About the footnote?

David hesitated for a moment.

"Yeah," he said finally. "It's about that."

I could hardly breathe. Mario had tried to warn me about this. "You can't bring anyone else's name into this," he'd said.

"See, there is the law like you do it up here," David said, motioning to the surroundings of my office, "and then there's the street law. On the street and in prison, it's a different set of rules. On the inside, legal technicalities don't matter." Through the vagaries of the prison system, other inmates had seen a copy of our recent habeas petition, with my footnote mentioning Joker. And word had spread that Mario had snitched. It didn't matter, in prison, that my footnote said the information had come from public police files.

When Mario recovered and returned from the infirmary to the general prison population, it would be only a matter of time before he was attacked again.

"What can we do? How can I help," I asked David.

"I'm not sure. Mario said he'll call you soon."

Mario called the next afternoon.

From clipped and roundabout conversations over the next few days, I learned that the only way to help Mario was to write a letter to a person on the outside, a former inmate who had influence among the Latino inmates in Calipatria, explaining that Mario had not said anything about Joker, and that the information about Joker had come from a witness statement in the police files, and that I had used it on my own initiative. This letter, along with the transcript of Mario's police interrogation, the witness statement from the police files, and our petition to the Court of Appeal, would be reviewed by the former inmate to determine whether Mario had snitched.

"This is *important*," Mario said, in what I took to be a big understatement.

I was drowning in billable work: depositions to prepare for, motions to draft, and masses of research. I had already been warned that my billable hours were low and that I needed to get them up. But that stuff would have to wait. This was a deadline of another kind.

I did not tell Bob Long or anyone else at Latham about the connection between the footnote and the stabbing, nor what I was doing to resolve the issue. This was solely my responsibility, to handle alone.

The letter and transcripts were delivered.

And then I waited.

Time ticked away. It was difficult to focus on my day-to-day work. My billable hours began slipping again. We were coming down to the last days that Mario would be in the infirmary before being put back into the general population, but all we could do was wait. Mario assured me he could handle himself until the "ruling" arrived, but I could tell he was anxious. And for good reason. A few weeks after he was released from the infirmary, he was attacked again. This time it was worse. He was stabbed thirteen times and one of his lungs was punctured.

A few days later, the ruling arrived in my office. My letter and its attachments had been reviewed carefully. The ruling contained a handwritten note that said, in carefully coded Spanish, that "legally" under the inmates' code, Mario had not snitched and that the attacks against him were unjustified.

Now I just had to get the note to Mario. I requested a meeting with him for the day he was to be released from the infirmary.

Prison guards check all papers handed to inmates, even those from attorneys. They would easily identify the note as a coded message. To camouflage it, and hoping the guards were inattentive, I printed more than five hundred pages of cases and marked some of them with handwritten marginalia. On a Wednesday in August 2005, though I was juggling demands for billable work from all sides, I skipped the office, told no one where I was going or why, and headed for Calipatria.

"WHAT'S THIS?" the prison guard asked.

My body went numb, and I hardly had enough air in my lungs to speak. I turned my head slowly and saw that he had parted the pages and was pointing his finger directly to the handwritten coded note. *Lie. Say something*, I thought.

"Oh, um, that's just a few of my notes to Mario about the cases," I blurted. I held my breath for a second, as the guard glanced down at the note. *I'm busted*, I thought. *I had failed Mario.* As I watched the guard's hands, waiting for him to reach for the handcuffs on his belt, another terrifying thought popped into my head: *Are they going to lock me up in* here?

After a beat, which seemed like an hour, the guard released the pages and the stack flopped back together, with the note still inside.

"Looks thrilling," he sneered.

As he unlocked the door separating my side of the room from the side where Mario sat behind a wire-reinforced glass partition, I slowly exhaled the breath I'd been holding. The guard walked through the door to Mario's side, relocking it behind him, and dropped the stack of papers on the desk in front of Mario.

When the guard turned his back to return to my side of the room, I caught Mario's eye. I smiled as I nodded at the stack and mouthed the words "it's in there." He smiled back.

I COULDN'T GET out of there fast enough. I could feel the color returning to my face as I pushed open the door to the outside. The heat didn't feel so bad. After retrieving my belongings from the check-in area, I walked quickly to my car, threw my suit jacket in the backseat, yanked off my tie, and drove out the front gate and onto the highway.

For a few minutes, I had visions of police cars chasing me down and dragging me back to the prison. But as the guard tower faded into the distance, I knew I was in the clear. I had never felt better or more exhilarated. No one but Mario and I knew about this. I felt like a hero.

Twenty miles later, however, the good feelings stopped cold. As I approached El Centro, my BlackBerry began to vibrate wildly. I had been out of range at the prison, and now a flood of emails and voice mails was pouring in. "Where are you?" my secretary had asked twice. Both her messages were marked urgent.

The partner on forty-four was asking where the hell his demurrer motion was. It wasn't due to be filed for another week, but he was leaving on a family vacation the next day and wanted to read it on the plane. Opposing counsel in a patent case wanted to discuss changing deposition dates and needed an answer immediately. The partner on forty-two wanted to know if he should forget about me and staff somebody else on his new case. "What's the status on the Rogs and RFAs?" another partner asked.

I pulled over in a rest area to peck out responses. I couldn't tell them what I was really doing, and I couldn't even say I was working on a pro bono case. The Associates Committee would be unforgiving about my priorities when it came to billable and unbillable hours.

"Got stuck in a meeting, I'll have the demurrer to you first thing in the morning," I told the partner on forty-four, knowing this would mean pulling an all-nighter after the four-hour drive back to the office. "Was in a meeting all day, I'll be in the office by four if you want to talk today," I told the partner on forty-two.

As I typed another response, a new email came in, this one from the head of the Associates Committee, saying he wanted to meet with me as soon as possible. He had stopped by my office, but I wasn't there, and, he pointed out, nobody seemed to know where I was. This could not be good. The formal reviews were coming up soon, and the only reason the Associates Committee would want to talk to me before then would be to discuss a problem.

—~—

CHAPTER 19

A Strongly Worded Decision

AUGUST–DECEMBER 2005

As I HEADED TO a sixth-floor conference room to meet with two partners from the Associates Committee, I knew this couldn't be good. It was widely known among associates that if two or more committee members attended your review, you were dead meat, or nearly so. Inside the room, positioned so I would be sitting across the long table from them, were Dan Goldman and David Moran, both partners on the Associates Committee.

Moran opened my file and began reading my reviews in a monotone, as if this were a normal review. The six partners I had worked for had all said positive things. As Moran read, I began to reflect on all the work I had done for the firm over the years: thousands of hours spent mindlessly reviewing documents, cutting and pasting discovery responses, proofreading edits, and researching case law.

The last review Moran read was from Bob Long. Bob praised

my work, noting that I had "made this case my own." He went out of his way to tell the committee that this was an important case, one that had attracted an extraordinary amount of priceless favorable publicity for the firm.

Moran then closed the file, looked up for the first time, and said, "Your message from the committee is as follows: Your billable hours remain below pace for the class of 2001. Failure to address this issue *will* negatively affect your future at the firm."

"Do you understand what this means, Ian?" Moran asked sternly.

I understood exactly what it meant. This was the formal language used to make a record for firing an associate if they did not immediately and dramatically shape up. It meant that, in a big and far-flung law firm, the record on paper of billable hours is the reality. Never mind the subjective evaluations, or the practical PR benefits the firm was getting from a case like Mario's. The only relevant evidence was in the billable hour spreadsheets. The firm was building a paper trail to fire me if I didn't bill more hours.

Moran continued: "Look, Ian. I spoke with your supervisors, and everyone speaks highly of you. But if you want to climb the ranks here, if you want to make partner, you have to make some better choices about your work."

It would have felt so good to quit right there. But the Court of Appeal's hearing in Mario's case was coming up in a couple of months. I had to hang on a little longer.

"Yes, I understand. I guarantee you it won't be a problem in the future," I said.

THE COURT OF APPEAL hearing in Mario's case took place on October 26, 2005. It was one of those magical days when everything falls into place. On the morning of the hearing, a front-page article about the case ran in the *Los Angeles Times* under the headline "In Search of Juvenile Justice." The article described Mario's writing talent and the chain of events that had brought the case to this point, portraying Mario in a very favorable light. The courtroom again was packed with Mario's family, friends, and supporters as Bob Long and I took our seats at a table in front of the panel of three justices. A young male deputy district attorney sat at the table next to us, while Joanne Lach watched from the gallery.

Each side had only thirty minutes—a half hour to present what we believed was Mario's last realistic chance. The Court of Appeal took judicial notice of the record from the Superior Court hearing before Judge Bowers, which meant our three justices* would be aware of the evidence and arguments we had presented before.

Bob Long went first, and he showed the difference between being merely good and being great. He was compelling and clear as he stood before the panel of justices, wearing his good-luck bow tie, and argued Mario's case. I was proud to be sitting at the table next to him. The three justices did not interrupt him once and appeared to hang on his every word.

The young deputy district attorney, who had recently taken over the case from Joanne Lach, did not fare so well. "It seems to me like what the court is interested in is narrowing the issues..." he began. The justices pounced on him.

*Appeals court judges are called justices in California.

"No. That's not right. We're interested in all of this," said one of them.

"What about Garcia's failure to investigate? What about the two shooters?" asked another.

"Is [Mario] right-handed or left-handed?" asked the third.

"I believe his mother testified that he is right-handed, but I think that's just a red herring," the deputy DA replied. The justice who asked the question visibly shook her head at the response.

The hearing could not have gone any better. But still we allowed ourselves only cautious optimism. We warned Mario and his family not to get their hopes up too much.

Every day I hoped the court would issue its decision and grant Mario a new trial. But as the days and weeks went by, the reality began to sink in that a new trial was still a long shot, that habeas corpus petitions almost never succeed, even on appeal, even when the case was compelling. After all, we had thought the evidentiary hearing with Judge Bowers had gone well.

If we lost again, it might be years before another court heard the case. I couldn't wait that long. I wanted badly to see it through to the end, but I needed to think about my future and start planning for a life after Latham. In a compromise with myself, I decided I could grit my teeth and stay at Latham until the Court of Appeal's decision arrived. But win or lose, that would be it. I was getting out.

THE ASSOCIATES COMMITTEE had spread the word among the partners that my hours were low and that I was available to take on any and all billable work. That made me fair game for them to pile it on. Almost immediately, I was assigned to two cases that were moving very quickly.

The first was a massive and complex patent dispute playing out fast in several courts in the United States and abroad. Two weeks earlier, a key senior associate on the case had left Latham. I was stepping cold into his shoes.

Within an hour of getting the assignment, documents from the case file nearly filled my office. These were followed quickly by a schedule of depositions to be taken and defended that looked like the Dodgers' season schedule: hundreds over the next three months, with "home" depositions in Los Angeles shaded in blue and "away" depositions in London shaded in red. I was to do all the preparation work for six depositions of our opponent's top executives, which would take place in Los Angeles one week after I first received the files. Then I was scheduled to take four depositions of technical witnesses in London a week later.

AT THE SAME TIME, I was assigned to a case defending a client who was being sued by the maker of a new drug for allegedly botching the drug's clinical trial. Latham had taken on the case only a few days earlier, after our client suddenly dropped its former lawyers—one week before the deadline for filing a key motion asking the court for summary judgment (to terminate the case in our favor without proceeding further).

And so, on the same Monday that I was assigned to prepare in one week six depositions in a highly technical patent case, I was also assigned to appear in the Napa County court that Friday to ask the judge to give us more time to prepare our summary judgment motion in our drug case. That motion was currently due the following Monday, the same day the depositions were to start in my patent case. For good measure, Tom Coleman, the lead Latham partner on the drug case, told me to have our summary judgment motion ready for filing the following Monday, in case the Napa County judge denied our request for more time. Drafting a summary judgment motion, by itself, would normally take two to three weeks.

Starting from scratch to prepare for six technically complex depositions, drafting a summary judgment motion for a different new case, and appearing in court in Napa, all in the same week, was going to take every waking minute; and I wasn't planning to sleep much. Hoping to find a draft summary judgment motion, or at least notes I could use, I looked through the stacks of files that our client's fired counsel had sent us. There was nothing I could use. I simply did not have time to do the motion. Since our chances were good that the judge would grant our request for more time to prepare the motion, I took a calculated gamble and put it on the back burner until after the hearing on Friday. If we lost, I would have to whip up the motion on Saturday and Sunday. I had no choice but to hope for the best on Friday and get cracking on my patent case.

The rest of that week, I worked frantically, reading through the patent case file, trying to parse out the technical issues, and searching through the hundreds of thousands of documents the parties had exchanged, looking for exhibits to use in the depositions. A small army of paralegals worked around the clock scanning documents into a software program that allowed me and other attorneys to perform Google-type searches for key words and names. And while this helped, a lot of my searches were turning up new documents—more than 100,000. I stayed at the office from Monday morning until late Wednesday night, downing pots of coffee and napping occasionally for a few hours on a couch on the sixth floor—under a photo of a lion mauling a gazelle. On Wednesday night, I finally went home, slept five hours, showered, and returned to the office to draft the deposition outlines. Finally, on Thursday afternoon, I sent outlines for the first two depositions to a paralegal who specialized in the technical and engineering aspects of patents and asked him to review my outlines, make any changes he thought appropriate, and send them on to the partner taking the depositions. Then I raced to LAX to catch a plane to Oakland, where I rented a car and made the one-hour drive to Napa.

My secretary had booked me a room at the five-star Silverado Resort in wine country, just a few miles from the courthouse in downtown Napa. Set at the end of a manicured, tree-lined drive, with a colonial estate–style main house and cabana-like rooms spread among the bucolic grounds and championship golf course, the accommodation would have given me a nice break from the office under different circumstances. But I was way too stressed to enjoy it. After checking into my cabana, I ordered room service and began preparing for the hearing the next day.

It is an old joke among seasoned trial lawyers that many big firm lawyers may have a reputation for winning cases in pretrial motions or settling them before trial, but "can't find the courthouse" for real trials. The next morning, I walked around the Napa town square for thirty minutes looking for the courthouse. I had the address and a map in my hand, but my only courtroom experiences up to this point had been in the big, serious-looking court building in downtown LA. In my stressed-out state, I overlooked the Victorian house at the center of the town square. In desperation, and with only minutes to go before the 8:30 A.M. hearing was scheduled to begin, I stopped someone who looked like a lawyer and asked him where the courthouse was. He looked at me strangely and told me I was standing in front of it. I followed him into the Victorian house and upstairs to Courtroom A.

The courtroom was much more intimate than I had expected. The elevated judge's bench took up half of the room. A handful of lawyers were crammed together in one pew only a few feet behind the lawyers' tables, waiting for their cases to be called. A uniformed bailiff stood in front of the judge's bench, and an elderly court reporter sat at a desk in the corner of the room, sandwiched between the witness stand and the wall. I took the last remaining space on the pew just as the judge emerged from his chambers exactly at 8:30 and the bailiff called the court to order.

My case was first up, and as I approached the lawyers' table, my nerves almost had me sweating through my shirt. Arguing motions in court was nothing new for me at this point, but I was exhausted and terrified by the thought of two more all-nighters writing a summary judgment motion if the judge denied us a continuance. The plaintiff's lawyer, a young partner from a big San Francisco firm, turned out to be the guy I had asked for directions in front of the courthouse. As I took my place at the table next to him, he said with a grin, "I see you found the place."

My strategy was to deflect all blame for the delay from my client and put it onto my client's former lawyers. Since their case file had given me absolutely nothing useful for the summary judgment motion, I had no qualms about pushing the former firm under a bus to try to gain a little sympathy for my client.

The hearing began ominously. The judge looked down at me, sitting almost literally at his feet, and began, "Mr. Graham, this case has been pending in my court for almost a year now. Why should I grant another continuance at this point?" Doing my best Bob Long impersonation, I replied earnestly, telling the judge that my client had diligently prepared for trial, but their previous counsel had only recently discovered a conflict of interest that prevented them from continuing their representation of my client. They had abruptly withdrawn, leaving my client in the lurch. And since Latham was retained as counsel only Monday, with summary judgment motions due a week later, we would not have an opportunity to take any depositions and we would have little time to review the file.

The plaintiff's lawyer opposed the continuance, hoping to force us to file a weak, doomed summary judgment motion. He basically called me a liar, saying there was no evidence to support my "conflict of interest" story, and painted my client as seeking to delay the trial by any means necessary.

After a little back-and-forth between the plaintiff's lawyer and me, the judge, perhaps noting the look of desperation on my face, granted the continuance. Staring down at me with his eyebrows raised, in what sounded more like a warning than a favorable ruling, he said that since I was a member of the state bar and an officer of the court, he would accept my statement, trusting that I would not mislead the court.

Whatever, I thought. Thank God! I would rather have spent the next two days in jail for contempt of court than writing that summary judgment motion. At least in jail I might have been able to sleep. As I left the courtroom, the plaintiff's lawyer stopped me in the hallway to apologize for his harsh words. "Just doing my job," he said.

I WENT BACK TO THE HOTEL and had two hours to kill before leaving for the airport. Although I had piles of work to do for the remaining depositions in my patent case and had to read and respond to the more than fifty emails that had come in while I was in court, I decided to leave my briefcase and BlackBerry in my room and have lunch on the hotel patio overlooking the golf course. I spent the next two hours sitting in the sun on a beautiful Friday afternoon, nursing my way through two glasses of cabernet and nibbling on a sandwich. I was so exhausted I could barely eat. As I watched the other guests wandering around the hotel in shorts and T-shirts, and the golfers happily three-putting on the eighteenth green, I wondered what these people did for a living. Many of them didn't look much older than I was. They were fit and tanned and seemed relaxed and at ease. I hadn't felt that way in years.

When I got back to LA that night, I decided to take the night off. I went to dinner with my girlfriend, Kate, but I fell asleep before 9:00 P.M. and she went out with some friends. She was twenty-six, beautiful, and worked in fashion at a job that, as far as I could tell, involved mostly shopping at Barneys and

Neiman Marcus. That was just fine with me. There were lots of lawyers at Latham who, despite their own unhappiness with their careers, only dated or married other lawyers. Proximity and limited options, it seemed to me, weren't the best building blocks for a relationship. Outside the office, I wanted to get as far from law as possible.

Although Kate and I got along well and had been dating for almost four months (a post–bar exam record for me), she couldn't understand what I did at the office all night or why I never had my weekends free. "What could possibly take you until two in the morning?" she asked with increasing frequency. But every time I mentioned quitting and doing something other than practicing law, she would scrunch her nose in an expression that said, "I don't think so!" She liked the house and the car and the material things my job provided. But even so, by this point, the idea of dating a lawyer was beginning to sour for her.

I spent Saturday and Sunday in the office finishing up the outlines for the remaining depositions coming up that week in my patent case. The next week, I spent my days in a conference room at the offices of opposing counsel in downtown San Diego, taking notes during the depositions and handing the partner taking the deposition exhibits as he needed them. At night, back at the hotel, I would stay up late writing summaries of the depositions for the client.

Then I had a week to prepare for the depositions I was taking in London.

On my return from London, when my plane landed at LAX, I was almost startled to hear the pilot signing off by wishing everyone a merry Christmas and happy holidays. In the last five weeks, I had been so busy I had hardly noticed that Christmas was only two days away.

For most associates, the days before Christmas and the week between Christmas and New Year's are a rare quiet time at the office. With clients' offices shut down for the holidays and many of the firm's partners on vacation, associates who have already racked up enough billable hours to qualify for their annual bonuses sneak away to relax for a few days before the billable hour count begins again on January 1. In the past, I had tried to clear at least the twenty-fourth and twenty-fifth of December to spend Christmas with my family, who had recently moved to Portland, Oregon, from D.C. But this year, because of my recent run-in with the Associates Committee and the two cases I was juggling, I was stuck in the office trying to catch up and to squeeze in every last billable hour before the end of the year.

MY PATENT CASE had kept me so busy over the past month that I hadn't even looked at my drug case since the Napa court had granted the continuance. I needed to catch up. Again, a lot of work had to be done in a short time. There were five boxes of discovery documents in my office, each containing more than a thousand pages to be reviewed and digested in preparation for depositions coming up in a couple of weeks, and I knew it would be slow going. The plaintiff's complaint was more than 120 pages long, with many exhibits. It was poorly written, which made it difficult to identify exactly what they were claiming our client had done wrong. The pharmaceutical industry jargon and the clinical trial procedures, while not quite as bad as analyzing patents, still made for heavy sledding. I was ready to spend the week between Christmas and New Year's reading and rereading the complaint and researching the legal arguments.

I ate Christmas dinner that year at an all-night diner in Santa Monica with another Latham associate who was stuck working over the holiday, too. We slumped in a booth and didn't say much to each other.

On the morning of December 26, loaded up on coffee, I pulled the first box of documents onto my desk and began reading.

IT HAD BEEN MORE than two months since the hearing on Mario's case in the California Court of Appeal, and I was getting antsy. As with Bowers, I figured the court would have ruled quickly if they thought Mario had been unjustly incarcerated. By now, I was becoming more discouraged than ever about our chance of success. Work was suffocating everything else in my life, and there was no end in sight.

Day to day, it was a dreadful time. But even so, driving to work every day past holiday decorations gleaming in the sunshine, I couldn't help but wonder if that day would be the one on which Mario would get his freedom. And that thought made me smile.

By midafternoon on December 28, my desk looked like an arts and crafts project. I had different colored tabs on hundreds of documents, sorted in various piles on my desk and on the floor according to relevance, date, and deposition witness. When my phone rang at around 3:30 P.M., I had a stack of papers on my lap, Post-it notes in my hands, and a pen in my mouth like a Cuban cigar. I thought about letting the call go to voice mail, but at the last moment, I reached back and hit the speakerphone button without checking the caller ID.

"Ian, can you believe it?" shouted a voice I recognized as a reporter from the *Daily Journal*, who had been closely following Mario's case. She sounded almost hysterical.

"Have you seen it? Did you get it? I just got it! This is so unbelievable!"

In an instant, I realized what she was talking about. I whirled my chair around to face my computer, sending papers flying off my lap. An email from the Court of Appeal sat at the top of my in-box. The subject line was "Action in Case BA 130020."

I told the reporter to wait a minute as I opened the email and quickly scanned to the last page of the ruling. The last two words, standing alone at the end of the page in bold type, said simply:

"PETITION GRANTED."

"No fucking way!" I shouted, temporarily forgetting about the reporter on speakerphone.

"Let me call you back after I read this," I told her, and hung up.

Without taking a breath, I picked the phone up and dialed a number I knew by heart: the state prison at Calipatria.

MARIO ROCHA SAT in his cell on the second level of the D block, reading another inmate's handwritten habeas corpus petition. In the last few years, as stories about his case had appeared in newspapers, he had become something of a celebrity in the Latino community. Other inmates sometimes came to him for advice about their own petitions. For a while he had enjoyed doing this, using legal knowledge gained from his case to help others. But recently he had tried to avoid being drawn into others' hopes. It made him think too much of his own case, something he had been trying not to do since the hearing in October. It was too painful to get his hopes up again. But the prison had been on lockdown for the past week, after an inmate had attacked a prison staff member. That it was Christmas seemed not to matter. Confined to his cell twenty-four hours a day, Mario had little else to do and no excuse for not reading other inmates' petitions.

When I reached the prison communications officer, he told me about the lockdown and made it clear that it would be impossible to get a call or mail through, or even to receive a call from Mario, until the lockdown ended, probably sometime the following week. I was bursting to tell Mario the news, and I wanted to tell the prison official the importance of the call. But Mario had warned me about telling *anyone* at the prison about his case. "Some of the guards are just as corrupt as the inmates," he had told me. And after Mario's stabbings, I had learned my lesson. So I kept my mouth shut.

It was disappointing that Mario would have to wait to hear the news, but there were many other calls to make. My boxes of drug trial documents would have to wait. The next two hours, which I spent on the phone with Mario's family, friends, and supporters, were the most rewarding of my life.

When I told Mario's cousin David the news, there was a long silence on the other end of the line. After a moment, I realized he was crying quietly. Finally, he thanked me and asked for a copy of the court's order for the family.

I tracked down Bob Long at his vacation house in Mammoth Lakes in the Sierras. He let out a loud whoop, overjoyed.

I called Sister Janet, who was speechless. In a very quiet but sincere voice, she said simply, "Ian, thank you."

As word of the ruling began to trickle out, calls began pouring in. The *Los Angeles Times* wanted a comment for a story they would run the next day. ABC News wanted information on the case. It seemed the whole country was taking notice.

As the impact of it all began to sink in, another thought crossed my mind: my career at Latham was over, on my terms.

We had hoped for a new trial, but the court's ruling exceeded our hope by vacating outright Mario's conviction, leaving it as though he had never been convicted. Unanimously and resoundingly, the court wrote that Mario's "trial counsel ignored petitioner's case for a prolonged period of time, made only desultory efforts, if any, to locate most witnesses and spent very little time in preparation of the case. This is such an extreme defalcation of the duty to conduct a timely and reasonable factual investigation of the case as to constitute a breakdown of the adversarial process."

CALIPATRIA PRISON finally ended its lockdown on New Year's Day 2006, a Sunday. Inmates could leave their cells for an hour in the morning and two hours in the early evening, although they were still not permitted to make or receive phone calls. Having been cut off from the outside world for over two weeks, Mario used his free time that evening to watch the news on a small television in another inmate's cell. As *ABC World News Tonight* began its final segment, announcing its "Person of the Week," Mario was surprised to see Sister Janet's face fill the screen. ABC was hailing her for her nearly ten-year effort to exonerate Mario Rocha, a young man she believed had been wrongfully convicted of murder as a sixteen-year-old in 1997 and sentenced as an adult to two life terms with no possibility of parole. Mario watched in disbelief as the ABC anchor concluded the segment: "Just last week, Mario Rocha's conviction was vacated by the California Court of Appeal in a strongly worded decision."

Mario sat motionless as the rest of the inmates in the room began to cheer and congratulate him. Their cheers soon turned into a full standing ovation from the entire cellblock. He could hardly believe it. His ten-year nightmare was ending.

—~—

CHAPTER 20

A Good Question

There is a strain of hubris that affects certain people in power...
It can cause right-thinking people to do terrible things.
The devil has a long tail.

—Tim Junkin, *Bloodsworth*

MARIO ROCHA was not alone.

In 1985, Kirk Bloodsworth was convicted of the brutal rape and murder of nine-year-old Dawn Hamilton, in Essex, Maryland. Bloodsworth was sentenced to death.

There was no physical evidence tying Bloodsworth to the crime. Four alibi witnesses testified that he was at home, far away from the crime scene, when the murder occurred. He was convicted largely on the basis of a description two eyewitnesses gave to a police sketch artist of a strange man lingering near the crime scene. The eyewitnesses—a ten-year-old and a seven-year-old—had described a man who roughly fit Bloodsworth's description.

After ten years in prison, Bloodsworth became the first person on death row to be exonerated by DNA evidence. The DNA found on Dawn Hamilton's clothing proved conclusively that Kirk Bloodsworth could not have committed the crime for which he had been convicted. He was innocent.

After Bloodsworth's release from prison, the Office of the State's Attorney issued a three-page press release describing in detail the evidence against him and stating that he was released because, as a result of the DNA test, his conviction now "lacked the necessary integrity." In her news conference, the state's attorney declined to say that Bloodsworth was innocent and offered no apologies. "There are no other suspects at this time," she said. "I believe he is not guilty, but I am not prepared to say he is innocent."

District attorneys have a difficult job. They deal daily with gruesome crimes and hardened criminals. They've heard every excuse in the book and have dealt with their share of sanctimonious defense attorneys. It is their job to find justice for crime victims and, in many cases, the grieving loved ones they leave behind, by putting the guilty behind bars. And they do all of this for much less money than they could be making if they switched sides to private practice.

But this proximity to crime has a hardening effect on some district attorneys. Defendants become dehumanized. The job of the DAs, and the advancement of their young deputies, too often comes to be about convictions more than justice. The state is their client, and by the time they get a case, the state wants a conviction. And if a conviction turns out to be wrong, the justice system is to be protected against embarrassment or liability, no matter what.

The loyalty to the lie, as Sister Janet calls it.

SHORTLY AFTER MARIO'S conviction was vacated by the Court of Appeal, the DA's office appealed to the California Supreme Court seeking to have the ruling overturned. When that failed, they quickly refiled charges against Mario for murder and attempted murder. They announced their intention to retry him.*

At this point, not a single shred of credible evidence remained implicating Mario in the shootings. Of the three eyewitnesses who testified against him at his 1997 trial, Lauro Mendoza admitted in court that he "wasn't sure" of his identification; Bryan Villalobos had officially recanted, writing out a sworn statement that he "never meant to identify Mario as a shooter"; and Matthew Padilla's identification of Mario as the driveway shooter, given a week after he had told the police he hadn't seen anything, was undermined by Laurie Nevarez's and Christina Aragon's statements that Padilla was in the backyard in a spot from which he could not have seen the shooter.

After the DA's office announced its intention to retry Mario, Marcus McDaniel met with Bobby Grace, the original prosecutor, and Pat Dixon, Grace's boss and the head of the DA's Major Crimes Division. McDaniel hoped to explain to them the lack of any evidence of Mario's guilt and to persuade them to drop the charges against him. It didn't go well.

*Technically, this would not have been a case of double jeopardy, as Mario had not been acquitted by a trial court.

"What new evidence do you have that he's innocent?" Dixon barked at McDaniel. Marcus tried to explain that in a case such as this, with no physical evidence, it was impossible to affirmatively prove innocence, and that in any event, it was the state's burden to prove guilt, not the other way around. And the point was there was no evidence of guilt. Dixon quickly interrupted him, saying that they still believed Mario was "good for" the murder and that if Latham couldn't prove he was innocent, the meeting was over.

Mario desperately wanted to get out of jail, and his family wanted badly to have him home. The DA's office knew that, and apparently they hoped to leverage the threat of a retrial to get Mario to cut a plea deal—to plead guilty to a lesser crime—that would allow the DA's office to save face. Although we never received a formal plea offer from the DA's office (not that Mario would have accepted it if we had), intermediaries informed us that the DA's office "might accept a manslaughter plea and only ten additional years in prison."

We filed a motion for bail to get Mario out of prison while the charges were pending. At the bail hearing before Superior Court judge Michael Pastor on July 28, 2006, Bobby Grace, the original prosecutor who had sent Mario to jail, opposed the motion. When it became clear that the judge was inclined to grant bail, Grace asked for $2 million, an amount that would guarantee Mario stayed in jail. Judge Pastor set Mario's bail at $1 million, still an amount no one thought could be raised.

But by then, Mario's case had made the papers, and a documentary about the case, *Mario's Story,* was playing at film festivals; it won the award for best documentary at the 2006

Los Angeles Film Festival. Mario's case was attracting attention and support. As word of his bail amount spread, checks began arriving at my office: fifty dollars here, one hundred dollars there, from a wide cross section of people. Associates and staff at Latham sent checks. A childhood friend of mine who had made it big on Wall Street sent $5,000. A couple of other well-heeled and generous supporters who had seen *Mario's Story* sent $10,000 each. Members of the board of directors of the InsideOUT Writers program (which Sister Janet had founded in Juvenile Hall) sent checks. Mario's family put in money and offered their homes as collateral. Within a few weeks, we had raised $60,000, enough for Chickie's Bail Bonds to guarantee the rest.

On August 25, 2006, Mario Rocha walked out of the Men's Central Jail and into the arms of his family, surrounded by friends and supporters. It was more than ten years after his arrest and incarceration, and eight months after the Court of Appeal had vacated his conviction.

I would have loved to watch Mario walk out of prison, but I was in Fresno that day, handling the exhibits in a meaningless deposition for a securities litigation case. I had tried to explain to the partner on the case what Mario's release meant to me, but all I got was a cold stare and a lecture about priorities.

That was it for me. I gave my two weeks' notice shortly afterward. This time there was no back-recruiting. Bob Long was retired. When I emailed him to say I was leaving the firm, he said simply, "I understand. This isn't for everyone." Teddy McMillan, who took me to lunch before my last day at the firm, was also understanding. "If you look around the firm, and there isn't a senior lawyer or partner you would want to emulate or consider a role model, then it's probably a good decision," he said. When I emailed David Moran, the partner on the Associates Committee, to tell him I was leaving, he replied simply, "Okay. Bye."

It felt strange to be leaving something that had occupied such a big part of my life for five years. Latham had become something of a second home to me. I knew which elevators ran the fastest, which conference rooms had their refrigerators stocked with drinks, and where the best spots in the library were to hide out and get some work done. But the cases and the deadlines that I had been juggling and that had kept me up at night had instantly been assigned to other associates and were no longer my concern. I was free just to walk out the door. Which I did, on a Friday afternoon, with a small box of personal items under my arm and a big smile on my face.

When I left Latham, in October 2006, only five of the forty-seven members of my first-year associate class of 2001 remained at the firm. Two of those left within the next six months.

FOR MORE THAN a year, the District Attorney's Office kept the charges pending against Mario and the threat of a retrial hanging over his head, limiting his employment opportunities and his ability to travel outside the state to attend the speaking engagements he was being offered. Although Bob Long was now retired, and I was no longer at Latham, we stayed involved in Mario's case, assisting two criminal defense attorneys, Mike Adelson and Joe Gutierrez, who were volunteering their services pro bono to help prepare for the retrial. Latham & Watkins continued to support Mario's case, paying for the services of a private detective for Adelson and Gutierrez.

Finally, on October 28, 2008, Bobby Grace announced to a crowded courtroom that the state was dropping all charges against Mario Rocha because they were "unable to locate some witnesses who originally testified against Rocha" and that as a result, they "could no longer move forward with the case."

Mike Adelson didn't let it go at that. "Before you is someone who many, many believe is factually innocent," he said to Judge Pastor. Pastor commended Mario for inspiring unwavering faith among the supporters who regularly filled his courtroom. "I have no doubt that you will go on to serve your friends and community in the future," the judge said.

Outside the courthouse, as Mario celebrated with his family and friends, Bobby Grace told a reporter covering the scene, "It isn't cut and dried by any means that he didn't do this."

Mario, however, remained humble. "For years, my story has become the story, but I am not the victim. The real victim is Martin Aceves."

IN THE FALL OF 2008, Mario, Sister Janet, Susan Koch (director of *Mario's Story*), and I were invited by the Sidwell Friends School in Washington, D.C., my alma mater, to be that year's Peace Speakers. We spent the entire day at Sidwell, speaking at assemblies for lower-, middle-, and upper-school students. It was a great experience for us to share our story with the Sidwell community, and we were warmly received by the students. The upper-school students, after watching the documentary *Mario's Story*, gave Mario an extended standing ovation.

But the most memorable moment of that day came in the morning, during our talk to the lower-school students. Speaking to a roomful of second-, third-, and fourth-graders, Mario broke down. As he talked about his life and his family, he began to cry and couldn't stop. It was as if a dam on the pain he had kept in check all those years had suddenly burst. The room fell silent and I thought, "This isn't going well." Then a tiny third-grade girl sitting in the front row raised her hand.

"Has anyone told you they were sorry?" she asked.

Mario pulled himself together and smiled at the girl. "That's a great question," he said. "Not yet."

POSTSCRIPT

IT WAS AN EMOTIONAL moment when finally I was able to reach Mario by phone after the lockdown, a few days after the Court of Appeal had vacated his conviction. By then he knew about the decision from the ABC News program.

I had spoken with the whole network of Mario's family and supporters: Sister Janet; his cousin, David; his mother, Virginia; Bob Long; Marcus McDaniel; the investigator, Aldo Velasco; and even with his once-skeptical aunt, Bertha. They had all come down to my office at Latham for a celebration.

Mario was ecstatic yet eloquent. "Everything has a purpose," he said. "The injustice brought those of us who believe in justice together."

Then he paused a long time and said, "Ian, it's been an honor to work with you."

"It's been an honor to work with you, too," I replied.

TODAY MARIO IS TWENTY-NINE. He is completing his sophomore year as a full-time undergraduate at George Washington University in Washington, D.C., where he was awarded a full scholarship. He is thriving in the university environment and he even claims to have enjoyed the required freshman courses.

He has also taken classes at UCLA as part of an eight-month Emerging Voices fellowship, awarded by PEN USA, an international organization of writers and free speech advocates.

He is active in speaking, counseling, and organizing in his home community.

He is still finding his way, between school, work, and social activism. His life is not without struggle. Those essential, formative teenager-to-young-adult years, when most of us have the chance to learn about life through trial and error, were taken away from him. But he remains bright, compassionate, open to the world around him, and eager to use his experience to help others and to be a voice for social justice.

Mario and I remain friends and are in frequent contact.

After leaving Latham, I briefly took a job at another law firm in Los Angeles. I had to see for myself whether my frustration with big firm law practice was the result of my experiences at Latham or if I was simply unsuited to that environment in general. Unequivocally, it was the latter. Associate life at a big firm is a well-paid, all-consuming grind that sharpens some of the brightest young legal minds by severely narrowing them. Based on my experience, and the experiences of my friends at other firms, I believe that for those who want to practice law in a big firm, Latham & Watkins is perhaps the best place to do it. Although during my time at Latham I was often frustrated by the nature of the work and the intense demands of the practice, in hindsight I realize how much I learned there and how much I grew as a person. In the end, big-firm law practice just wasn't for me. As a big-firm lawyer, you don't cure anyone, you don't build anything, you don't create or own anything. You are a middleman, dedicating your life to resolving the problems of, or enriching, corporations. Or at least it seemed that way to me.

For those who truly enjoy the intellectual challenge of this kind of law practice, it is, I imagine, rewarding work. I got into it for the wrong reasons and found out I didn't enjoy day-to-day big firm practice. The difficult part was getting out. Leaving behind a prestigious job and steady six-figure paycheck was a difficult thing to do. Mario's case was my personal salvation—in the short term, because my emotional investment in the case was what enabled me to survive the grind at Latham for five years; and in the longer term, because the case unlocked the golden handcuffs and freed me to see a world and a life beyond the confines of a big law firm.

I STILL LIVE in the little house in Santa Monica, on a much tighter budget. It's a trade-off I understand now and am happy to make. I worked again with Susan Koch, the producer of *Mario's Story,* as associate producer of her latest documentary, *Kicking It,* about a group of homeless soccer players who made it to the Homeless World Cup. I'm on the board of InsideOUT Writers, the group Sister Janet started, which teaches creative writing in juvenile detention facilities. I've been speaking at law schools and public-defender organizations, when I wasn't busy writing this story.

CPSIA information can be obtained
at www.ICGtesting.com
Printed in the USA
LVHW092357150819
627878LV00001B/14/P